CW01657955

# ODD MAN OUT

*By the same author*

THIS IS MY STORY

PILGRIM'S PROGRAMME

THE PLAIN MAN LOOKS AT HIMSELF

THE PLAIN MAN LOOKS AT THE COMMANDMENTS

HIM WE DECLARE (with the Bishop of Coventry)

ONWARD CHRISTIAN SOLDIER: The biography of Sabine Baring-Gould

WOODBINE WILLIE: The biography of G. A. Studdert Kennedy

FISHER OF LAMBETH: The biography of Archbishop Fisher

BRITISH POLICE IN A CHANGING SOCIETY

NO OTHER GODS

THE CHRISTIAN AND RETIREMENT

A COMMUNICANT'S MANUAL

BEREAVEMENT

EUTHANASIA

A TIME TO DIE

PILGRIM'S ENGLAND

# Odd Man Out

*a biography of Lord Soper of Kingsway*

by

WILLIAM PURCELL

MOWBRAY
LONDON & OXFORD

*Copyright © William Purcell, 1972, 1983*

ISBN *0 264 66906 1*

*This paperback and revised edition*
*published 1983 by A. R. Mowbray & Co. Ltd,*
*Saint Thomas House, Becket Street,*
*Oxford, OX1 1SJ*

*(First published 1972 in hardback as 'Portrait of Soper')*

*All rights reserved. No part of this publication may be reproduced, stored in a retrieval system, or transmitted, in any form or by any means, electronic, mechanical, photocopying, recording, or otherwise, without the prior permission in writing from the publisher, A. R. Mowbray & Co. Ltd.*

*Printed in Great Britain by*
*The Thetford Press Ltd, Thetford, Norfolk*

**British Library Cataloguing in Publication Data**

Purcell, William
Odd man out.
1. Soper of Kingsway, Donald, *Baron*
I. Title
287'.1'0924 BX9225.S/
ISBN 0-264-66906-1

For Margaret,
A daughter of the Manse, and my dear wife

# Contents

# ACKNOWLEDGEMENTS

MANY PEOPLE have helped with advice and guidance and information during the writing of this book, and their variety is some indication of the width and interests and connections possessed by the man who is the subject of it. But the author would wish to express his particular gratitude to the following: the Revd Dr Eric Baker; the Revd Dr Harold Roberts; the Revd Dr Colin Roberts; the Revd Stewart Denyer; the Revd David Mason; the Revd Derrick Greeves. The Rt Hon. Harold Wilson, PC, MP, and Michael Foot, MP, were kind enough to speak about Donald's political activities; Lady Serota contributed invaluable reminiscences of his time as an Alderman of the London County Council, later the Greater London Council. Mrs Margaret Marshall, at one time Lord Soper's secretary, was most helpful in the matter of press cuttings, Miss Sheila Townson, Warden of the Katherine Price Hughes Hostel in the West London Mission, generously allowed use of her unique collection of tape recordings of Donald Soper's speaking through the years. George C. Hunter III, Director, New Life Missioners, of the Board of Evangelism of the United Methodist Church, USA, very kindly supplied a copy of his PhD thesis upon the work of Donald Soper. Mrs Millicent Lawrence, Donald's sister, supplied invaluable information on the home background. Mrs R. S. Lloyd, formerly Sister Lottie Hudd, recalled war years at the West London Mission; Sister Lewis, now a social worker in South London, supplied first-hand information and reminiscences of the Order of Christian Witness, and Mr Jack Kirby, a Londoner born and bred and, with his brother, a faithful attendant for many years of Donald upon Tower Hill, recalled, as probably no one else could have done, the atmosphere of those remarkable outdoor gatherings. All these, and many others, in many walks of life, have been kind enough to answer questions about one whom they all knew—Donald Soper.

I am grateful to the *Observer*, *Methodist Recorder*, *British Weekly* and *Tribune* for kindly giving me permission to quote extracts from their papers.

# Preface to this Edition

ANY STUDENT of the media, especially radio and television, will know how prominent a part Donald Soper, Lord Soper of Kingsway, continues to exercise upon the public scene. His story is therefore very much a living one, and it is good that those who were not even born when it began, should be able from this narrative to share the deep interest of it, and to learn something of the record of this great though always unassuming man.

W.P.

# Preface

IN CASE it should be wondered why an Anglican should attempt to write of a distinguished Methodist so close a study as this book endeavours to be, it may be well to set down the reasons. The first is the interest and admiration which the subject of this book has stirred in the writer of it over many years. The second is the regard which the writer has had, over an even longer length of time, for the Methodist people—a regard reinforced by many contacts with them in the production of religious broadcasting programmes. This regard has also been nurtured by personal ties. An Anglican who married the daughter of a Methodist minister can scarcely regard himself as a stranger either to the ways or to the history of the people called Methodists. But chiefly this book has been written because, for the writer of it, Donald Soper personifies that Christianity in action which in all times, and especially now, is so greatly to be admired because it is strong, consistent, totally unecclesiastical, bigger than any church, and extending always out into the world.

WILLIAM PURCELL

# Preface

# Introduction

WHEN WILLIAM PURCELL approached me with a view to his writing this book, he made it clear that he wished the work to be done in close association with me. So we have talked much together, and he has shown me the results as he has set them forth. This book reflects, therefore, some of the product arising from a personal encounter, throughout which he has had my entire confidence. I have expressed myself freely to him, as indeed have many of my friends whom he has diligently sought out. Obviously, he has been at liberty to say what he wishes and therefore it is fair to point out that the views he expresses are his own. If in the result this verbal portrait may seem not to show enough warts, as I have occasionally suggested to him, then that is his doing, not mine. He has taken me as he has found me, and his patient reconstruction of the background of my life's journey to date, combined with the personal association of which I have spoken, makes me able to affirm that this, so far as I am concerned is, without prejudice to any other, past, or even to come, the definitive biography of myself.

SOPER

I

# Tower Hill

ON MOST Wednesdays at 12.30, winter and summer, fair or foul, an event has taken place on Tower Hill, in the City of London which, by reason of long continuance, has become something of a ritual. Donald Soper, or the Reverend Lord Soper of Kingsway, baron and life peer, addresses, argues with, and is often heckled by whatever crowd he can collect. The crowd is usually large, often curious, and by no means always altogether friendly. He has been doing this since 1926, only occasionally prevented from keeping an appointment which he obviously places high among the priorities of a busy life. Who exactly the appointment is with is not altogether clear. It could be with the crowd; it could be with God, since he tends to speak of the things of God, skilfully intermingling them with those of Caesar. It could even be with himself, as though it were some inner compulsion which drives him, year after year, to so arduous an assignment. This question of motivation is difficult, and one of the reasons which he himself has given for this weekly, verbal all-in wrestling bout does not seem, when compared with the reality of the event itself, to be wholly adequate.

'The underlying conviction which prompted me to adventure myself upon the Hill was the certainty that Christianity is the real focus-point of all our questioning and that in it can be found the answer to every problem that vexes human kind. It is the complete world view. For me the teaching of Jesus, that all peoples belong to the family of God, and all things can become part of the furniture of God's home, is the truth which makes us free. In it, the apparent antitheses are reconciled, purpose and significance are everywhere discoverable, and nothing is trivial.'[1]

The language seems stilted in comparison with the knockabout nature of the event on Tower Hill and with the obvious originality of the man at the centre of it. And then, a little later in the same book, there is something quite different, something which humanises the matter straightaway. 'Tower Hill on Wednesday, or on any other day for that matter, isn't full of minds walking about and arguing with each other; it's full of people. It wasn't a brain that interrupted me last week and called me a "twister"; it was Mr James Wilson, of 12 Beanbody Buildings, London, E.5, who not only has mental objections to the theology I happened to defend, but is also happily married, enjoys a local reputation as a free thinker, but sends his children to Sunday School, supports Chelsea, can pick out "Love's Old Sweet Song" on a piano with enthusiasm and with a stabilised bass note, has a passion for gardening and trouble with his wife . . . and Mrs Wilson could tell you still more about him.'[2]

The contrast is interesting. In the first quotation he is talking about concepts; in the second about people, and there is plenty of evidence in this man's story to suggest that it is there, close to humanity on equal terms, giving himself and giving and taking the knocks, that he is, and has been these many years, at his best.

The course of events, on Wednesdays on Tower Hill when he is speaking, may have become something of a ritual. But it is a striking one. What happened on one Wednesday in the early spring of a recent year may be taken as a sample. By 12.15 there was no sign of anything portending. The scene was familiar; a wind out of the north-east, occasionally bringing sleet. The turreted mass of the Tower lay beside the Thames. Tourists, even so early in the year, were already about the place, camera-hung, looking at the Yeoman Guards in their Tudor rig.

But, separated totally from tourism, across an open space—that very one where in times past often the scaffold had stood

[1] Donald Soper, *Tower Hill, 12.30* (Epworth Press, 1963). [2] Ibid.

and the axe fallen—there was in preparation a purely London occasion. Obviously, this one was for the locals. In an area flanked by Byward Street to the north, and the church of All Hallows to the west, a snack bar was already serving a queue of workers, all men. They could have come from the warehouses and offices around. Some of the faces might have interested Chaucer, like that of a gap-toothed man in a dirty cap who grinned at everything for no reason, or the bitter face of a small man wearing a GPO badge, who scowled with equal persistence. Behind them, one of those curious characters whose street speciality it is to have themselves handcuffed, fettered, chained, tied up in canvas and then, for the public entertainment, to extricate themselves, was preparing for his act. But this, clearly, since most ignored it, was not the main event expected.

This main event began at 12.30 when a man appeared and took up a position at the foot of the speaker's rostrum which one of his companions had unfolded against the wall bordering the eastern end of the space. The newcomer caught the eye. Difficult to place, he could have been anything from a distinguished journalist to a politician visiting his constituency. He wore a white raincoat over a light suit; collar and tie. Wings of white hair were tightly brushed back on each temple. The features were very sharp. Deep lines, possibly indicative of strain, ran from the nose to the corner of the mouth. The gap-toothed man eyed him. The bitter man offered a remark, to those standing near, that he, this man by the rostrum, newly arrived, 'had never done a bloody day's work in his life'. And then, at 12.30 precisely, just as the escapologist was having his chains fixed, the speaker climbed on to his rostrum.

'I have come here', he began, in a gravelly yet cultured voice, 'to offer a few reasoned arguments, to those who like a reasoned argument, which might help us towards making Christian judgements upon some of the events of the day.'

The gap-toothed man grinned. The bitter man scowled even more. The Reverend Donald Soper was again in action on

Tower Hill. Forty minutes later he was still there, and having a rough time. The crowd by then had grown greatly, spreading backwards on to the escapologist's pitch. The sleet had increased: the man on the rostrum, bareheaded, stood and endured it. He endured the heckling with the same air of practised stoicism as though he had seen all this before, and worse. The gap-toothed man and the bitter man, having now gathered a claque of supporters, stood just beneath him to his left. When they interrupted, which was often, the speaker looked ahead, impassive, occasionally changing his stance to intervene, or to continue a more reasoned discussion with someone on his right. Even so, the going for him was clearly hard, the scene for the spectator even painful, so that it was possible to feel for the man and at the same time to wonder why he did it.

Why did he, indeed? Who was he, anyway? These problems clearly exercised two young Canadians who had wandered over from the tourist area to investigate this unscheduled spectacle. They wore maple leaf badges on their anoraks. Puzzled, genuinely inquiring, they were young enough to be the offspring of parents who could themselves have been just coming into the world when Donald Soper first began to speak on Wednesdays on Tower Hill. The possibility may give some idea of the immensity, in terms of persistence, of the achievement. He was there, in the mid-thirties, when the age of illusion, like a train packed with arguing passengers, was plunging towards the tunnel of 1939–1945. He was there, having queer, off-the-cuff arguments about the shape of the soul, or the nature of heaven, or whether man could be a Christian in a capitalist society, when Hitler was rearming, Mussolini posturing, Edward VIII abdicating, and pacifists, than whom few were more dedicated than he, passionately disputing. He was there when men were dying in the Spanish Civil War. He was there when Abyssinia was raped and the League of Nations died. He was there when an old man descended upon Munich, carrying an umbrella.

He was there, or at any rate, not far away, through the phoney war. He was around, unshaken in his pacifism, through Dunkirk and the Battle of Britain, and all the blood, sweat and tears which ensued. He was around in the Attlee age, through the days of the end of Empire and of the beginnings of the Welfare State, through the Conservative administrations following, through the death of a king, and the still-birth of a second Elizabethan era. He was there when the first H bomb blew up Bikini Atoll. He was there during Korea, Suez, Vietnam, through the arguments about free dentures on the Health Service and, always as a recurrent undertone, through the repetitive questions as to whether heaven was a place or as to whether a man could prove God. Like some indefatigable barker in the great tragi-comic road show of Vanity Fair he has gone on and on, convinced that he is doing the right thing, if not always managing to say it.

The origin of it all he has himself put on record.

'To me Tower Hill was but a name, until from Theological College I was appointed as a Methodist probationer to the South London Mission in the Old Kent Road. One day a young fellow of my congregation, who worked in the City, came to me much exercised in his mind. He went each dinner time to Tower Hill, and among the various speakers to whom he listened he was as impressed by the incisive and the measured arguments of the Catholic Evidence Guild as he was dissatisfied with the fatuous and petulant explosions of the many so-called Protestant advocates. Was there not an intellectual case for the faith which he heard from the Methodist pulpit Sunday by Sunday? Could not we defend the things dear to us reasonably and persuasively? He was sure that he spoke for many others who felt that much religious propaganda on the Hill was a waste of time and most ineffectively done. . . . The critics were left unanswered, and yet surely there were answers. . . . Would I have a go at it? I readily agreed. We promised to meet on the next Tueday. Had I known as much of the Hill as I do now I should probably not have agreed so glibly to put matters right.'

That was a long time ago. By this time, like the wedding

guest after his encounter with the Ancient Mariner, he is a wiser, if not necessarily a sadder man. Certainly, his emphasis today seems less on the evangelistic side. Nevertheless, the elements of the situation remain: the courage required; the persistence needed; and the basic question of the two young Canadians, 'Who is he?' None of the answers given there, on the spot, among the crowd, seemed to yield any satisfaction. They could hardly be expected to, since all were part of an infinitely greater whole: the character of Donald Soper, at once a public figure and a notable Christian leader in an age which is not rich in leaders, and a man whose ministry may yet turn out to be, in its total involvement with the common life and equally total abandonment of the protective mechanisms usually surrounding the office, prophetic of the time when the Christian Church may have returned to the places where first its voice was heard: the street corner.

But who is he? Lord Soper, certainly. Created a life peer in 1965, he was the first of his kind to enter the House of Lords. A Methodist minister, appointed to the South London Mission in 1926, to the Central London Mission in 1929, he was in 1936 appointed Superintendent of the West London Mission with its headquarters at Kingsway Hall. There, to quote a writer in the *British Weekly* of 1969, he 'for more than 30 years has offered the whole of Christendom and the world at large a sustained witness to Christian truth'. He was in 1953 President of the Methodist Conference and thus the recipient of the highest honour that Church can bestow upon one of its ministers. He has been throughout a Socialist and a pacifist. The left wing, at any rate, of the Socialist Party, has long held him as a supporter. As a Socialist, he was Alderman of the London County Council and later of its successor, the Greater London Council. His Cambridge college, St Catharine's, elected him an Honorary Fellow in 1966. Yet, when all these dry facts have been recited, no one is the slightest bit nearer to any understanding of this complex and extraordinary character. Any answer, in fact, to the question as to who exactly Donald Soper is would have to go a good deal further than the recitation of facts about him. It is essential to note what he has done, what he has said about himself and about others and, especially, what others have said about him.

Inevitably, he has often been involved in controversy, particularly within the area of his pacifism. A long-remembered instance took place at the Methodist Conference of 1950, Dr Sangster being President. The incident is described by Norman Goodall, at that time Press Officer of the Methodist Church. 'The Korean War was at its height and one afternoon, just as the session broke for tea, Dr Soper said that Communism would be preferable to war. Such a statement at that time was more remarkable than it would be now, but I was besieged in the corridors by anxious ministers and others.'[1]

But Soper's pacifism, a life-long commitment, is another tale and must wait. So, for that matter, must any account of the numerous other causes—almost always minority causes—which he has supported. Like the man of La Mancha, he has tilted at plenty of windmills in his time. Whether they have in fact been windmills—or whether they have been, and are, real evils, is a question as puzzling as the world in which they have arisen. It could be that this particular Don Quixote has often enough been right while the rest of us have been wrong, or at any rate complacent. So, from the League Against Cruel Sport to the Campaign for Nuclear Disarmament, Soper has been involved and is now. In the years of the Aldermaston Marches, he was generally to be found in the front rank, and the Press pictures of the time hold him there, eccentrically clad in his uniform of black cassock surmounted by worn leather jerkin.

What does he think about himself, in so far as he thinks about himself at all? The *Observer*, in its week-end supplement, came up with a Soper self-assessment in a series in which people were asked to name their favourite colours. A psychiatrist interpreted the choice in terms of character. The subject was then

[1] Quoted in Paul Sangster's *Dr Sangster* (Epworth Press, 1962).

asked to comment upon the interpretation. Soper chose red, yellow, blue, green, black and violet. The comments, both his and the psychiatrist's, are worth giving in some detail.

Soper's choice of red and yellow was, according to the psychiatrist involved, the mark of a complete extrovert, one who 'seeks success, stimulation and a life full of experience. Likes contact with others and is enthusiastic by nature. Receptive to anything new, modern or intriguing; of many interests.'

Soper said: 'I've always been ambitious. I wanted to be a very good minister of the Gospel, and I never wanted to be anything else—though in the early days I had very few qualifications, spiritual or otherwise. But I've always been an extrovert so this didn't really bother me. No, I don't think it's a disadvantage: it depends how you use your extrovert qualities. The person like myself who becomes more involved in what's going on around him is no worse, I would say, than the parson who is more concerned with his own ego and *amour propre* than with the responsibilities of his own position. . . . The way I approach my duties drives me out into the open air, into the sort of atmosphere represented by Speakers' Corner—where I had been speaking on Sunday afternoons for more than forty years—or Tower Hill. I had never been content to practise my religion within purely spiritual boundaries, and I found myself very much involved in politics because I have what you might call a radical approach to social problems. . . .

'Yes, I certainly am interested by new ideas, whether new developments in evangelism, in the Church, or in science and politics.'

Further appraisals of his colour choice (blue and green as third and fourth choice) suggested that he 'acts in an orderly, methodical and self-contained manner', but brown and grey suggested that he was 'willing to become emotionally involved . . . but tries to avoid conflict'.

Soper's comments on this were: 'I've made myself orderly . . . as for conflict, well, I don't like conflict for conflict's sake, but

I'm by no means thin-skinned. I enjoy controversy. I enjoy argument. Yes, it would have to be admitted that I like getting my own way.'

The article suggested that his putting black and white last inferred he was suffering from 'stress resulting from unwelcome restriction or limitation' and that he 'wants to act freely and uninhibitedly, but is restrained by his need to have things on a rational, consistent and clearly defined basis'.

Soper said: 'I have a bad arthritic hip, and I do indeed fret about that and other physical infirmities. For the rest, there is a good deal in what is said. I am quite sure I wouldn't believe in anything which I can't reconcile with my reason. My own thinking, I suppose, is a variant of the idea that socialism in this country—practical, radical-thinking—depends more on Christian principle than what we are pleased to call a "scientific" basis, that we owe more to the tradition of Methodism than we do to Marx'.[1]

The remark places him accurately in context. For Soper, clearly, his Methodism is central to all he is and does. No way to any understanding of him seems possible without the use of that key, even though some within his own Church have held at times that the key did not fit. Others, however, within the same tradition, have thought differently. Two views of Soper, the one from a senior Methodist, the other from one of a different and later generation, are interesting. Eric Baker, for many years Secretary of Conference, one of the few permanent officials which the Connection allows itself, spoke, among other things, of this kind of love-hate relationship between Methodism as a whole and Donald Soper over the years.

'Everybody loved him, and even the individuals who disliked him most succumbed to his charm when they met him. And yet his fearless espousal of unpopular causes, and causes which they disagreed with, has meant sometimes that he has suffered very severely—almost ostracism. I think the occasion when in Con-

[1] The *Observer* colour supplement (8 March 1970).

ference he said that it would be preferable for the Russians to overrun this country than that we should retaliate with force; or when he spoke of how impossible it was to be a Conservative if one was to be a truly Christian disciple (a saying which, of course, has been very much misunderstood and rather woodenly misinterpreted by all sorts of people) were instances of his sometimes provocative statements. I don't think that there can be any doubt that this part of his make-up did result in the delay in his election as the President of Conference. He did receive this honour in 1953 and he was as young at that time as any President had ever been. But perhaps he would have received it at rather an earlier stage, I'm quite sure, if he had not had within him those particular streaks of belief and behaviour which alienated some people from him. But his intrinsic greatness and ability and his heroic devotion to the Christian cause, the out-of-doors ministry on Tower Hill and, later, the ministry at Hyde Park, which was not matched or even approached by anybody else at all, meant that, as it were, even the ranks of Tuscany could scarce forbear to cheer.'

But this ambivalent relationship with his own communion had its origins, it seemed, further back. Baker continued: 'Donald very early received the complete approval of all the Methodists with whom he came in contact. He was in danger of being—and I use the word danger advisedly—the darling of the Connection. He was a man of almost unequalled charm among the young Methodist ministers, and he had so many gifts, both sacred and secular, that he was greatly sought after in many quarters. It could be said that the Establishment—and I use that word in no bad sense—fell for Donald in a big way and would liked to have captured him for their own ends, which were, from a Methodist conventional point of view, very admirable and splendid ends.

'It is, however, to Donald's eternal credit that though he was by no means one who was unwilling to be popular—he enjoyed being popular—and though he is much more sensitive than most people would think, and feels very definitely hurt if people disapprove of him, yet he resisted what must have been a very severe temptation to yield to the opportunities that he had of becoming a kind of favoured son of the Establishment. Instead, his growing understanding and appreciation of Christian truth meant that, if he was to be true to it, he had to come out in opposition to many conventional ideas that were held, and he had to espouse causes that were unpopular on some occasions, with the majority of his fellow Methodists. He did not hesitate to do this, though it cost him very often the approval of people, and meant that he had to follow a lone path and incur the displeasure of people whose goodwill he would have been very glad to have.'

Another kind of comment on Soper, speaking more of his impact on the world now than on his Church yesterday, came from a man called David Mason. It was necessary to go into London's Notting Hill to find him; into that dubious inner-city area where so many social tensions seem to vibrate in the very air. Mason was vigorous and determined, like a man who knew what he was about, believed in it, and was enjoying it. His phone rang often. 'Could be those Black Power people again. . . .' He said he was used to it. He wore a roll-neck sweater, and was a Methodist minister. He began by linking Soper to the situation he himself was in, there in Notting Hill. 'Round about 1958 a number of younger Methodist ministers, of whom I was one, were thinking in terms of starting an experiment in group or team ministry, here in this country. I had witnessed a team ministry in an East Harlem Protestant parish of New York, and had been reading very carefully the work of the French and Catholic worker priests. I and others had felt the desperate need in British Methodism to try and reproduce some of their insights and ideas and actual working methods. We had prepared a memorandum which we hawked round various Methodist officials, most of whom read our work but were not ready to act on it. It so happened that in 1958 there were the

Notting Hill race riots, which stirred the national conscience, and led to Donald Soper a few months later making a passionate plea, at the Methodist Conference, for a new approach in the inner City, such as Notting Hill, by the Methodist people. I immediately sent to him a copy of our memorandum on team ministry. He rang up the same day as he got it and said yes, this was the kind of thing he had been looking for when he made his speech at Conference, and this was the kind of work he would like in Notting Hill, and when could I begin? So the experiment in Notting Hill, in team ministry, in growing a Christian Church from the grass roots in a multi-racial area, was a result of Donald Soper's speech at Conference and of the fact that he promised Conference himself that he would take the pastoral and financial responsibility for this. He became Superintendent Minister for the Notting Hill experiment from 1960–67, and during the whole of that seven years, when things were extremely difficult, when there was violence, when we were short of money, when there were many headaches, jealousies from other Christians, and resentments from local politicians, Donald Soper was always there in the background. Without him the Notting Hill experiment just would not have got off the ground. I think it illustrates his immense moral courage, that when other prominent Church leaders agreed intellectually but lacked the courage and the will to act, Donald Soper made good this deficiency.'

But the influence of Soper on this man, it seems, stretched much further back. He said: 'I first met Donald Soper in the summer of 1942. At that time I was only sixteen, a schoolboy in the sixth form at Mercer's School in the City of London. This was the height of the war against Hitler and, like many other schoolboys at that time, I was faced with the prospect of call-up at eighteen, and was trying to make up my mind what to do. I was at the time feeling my way towards pacifism, finding it a very hard position to adopt because of the emotion engendered at the height of the war and because of being such a small minority group, with very little public discussions and expression of its point of view. And, because of my interest in pacifism, I was beginning to become interested in Christianity. I started to attend a sort of pacifist young persons' discussion group, and by coincidence the secretary of this group was a young girl who was a member of Soper's church at Kingsway Hall. She mentioned there was a public meeting in Trafalgar Square the following Sunday afternoon in order to plead that the blockade of Hitler's Europe should be lifted to some extent, to allow relief supplies.

'There was quite a number of interesting speakers, but Donald Soper towered above them. What intrigued me was that he claimed, though he didn't look like it, to be a parson; and that his church was just up the road from Trafalgar Square. So, the following Sunday, I started to go and continued to go regularly for many a long year afterwards.

'How did he influence me? Well, first of all he influenced me to offer for the Methodist ministry, and myself to become a committed Christian. He influenced me greatly in my thinking because of his unusual combination of different strands of churchmanship. For example, he seemed to have in those days, probably still has, a very liberal theology and yet, at the same time, a very catholic churchmanship. He combined a very sceptical attitude on more peripheral doctrines such as the virgin birth, with a very deep personal commitment to sacramentalism, to the Eucharist, and to traditional Church worship and in that sense, to traditional Church theology. But I think it is particularly his style of life as a Christian minister that captured my imagination; that he was, in Dick Sheppard's words, a "human parson". He had none of the pomposity or the reserve of any of the stereotypes. He had a great sense of humour; he was free and easy; he was acceptable. All this fired my imagination. Now that I myself am a minister, and can measure his ministry against my own experiences over the years, I can see just how significant and great is the style of Christian minister that he has hammered out.

'It is easy to underestimate him; easy to think of him just as a great open-air orator, as a leading pacifist and socialist, and fail to see the other side of his personality. For example, he gives up an amazing amount of time, any day, every day, to people who want to see him, often at extremely short notice or no notice at all. He has a very deep concern for people in their personal life who are going through a time of trouble. And many months or years later, when they themselves had forgotten what it was that troubled them at the time, he would discreetly ask whether they are safe at the other side. Knowing Donald Soper, too, has led to a pattern of churchmanship I have never surrendered. I have learned from his example that an effective Christian minister is one whose first congregation is the non-churchgoer, and that the real role of the Christian minister is to communicate with and to speak of the Gospel to people who have little or no connection with the organised Church. It led also to a belief that Christian ministry must find expression in the political field, and that if there is no sort of political result from Christian thinking and Christian theology and Christian churchmanship, then there is something gravely wrong.

'I think he is much underestimated in the Methodist Church as in the Christian Church as a whole. He is an extremely humble man, with a side to his personality that is often not appreciated by those who know him only in public life; a man with a very profound and deep and hidden spirituality; to whom, to celebrate the Eucharist or to lead worship is the most satisfying thing that he can do. He is a man who, if he had gone into any other walk of life, whether politics, university, business, or perhaps the Bar, would undoubtedly have come to the head of his profession. But he chose to become a Methodist minister in the 1920s and has never really regretted that choice. And if he were to begin all over again, even now, I feel myself that he would be content to be an ordained Christian minister and would still see this as the most exciting vocation that anyone could follow.'

Here, then, is a man of his times and a man of his Church,

though much bigger than the latter in the sense that Soper has made an impact upon a far wider world than that of Methodism only. And though, as has been said, Soper would not have been what he is without his Church, yet it is difficult to fit him into any part of the traditional pattern of it. To quote Eric Baker again: 'Some have said of Donald Soper that he is the greatest Methodist since John Wesley. That seems to me a judgement that can neither be upheld nor denied. It depends so much on what is regarded as greatness. Certainly, there has been no greater Methodist than Donald Soper in the particular kind of contribution it has been his delight and ability to make. But who can say, for example, whether Donald, who in his own field is absolutely supreme, is greater than Scott Lidgett, of whom similar things can be said, though in a quite different field.'

But a difficulty arises at this point. Any endeavour to arrive at some picture of a man necessarily involves trying to place him in the background and framework characteristic of his kind. Yet with Soper the attempt is bound to fail simply because he seems to differ so widely, both in character and method, from some, if not all, of his contemporaries within his own tradition. If he is compared, for instance, with two of the most distinguished Methodist ministers of his own day, Leslie Weatherhead and William Sangster, the point immediately becomes clear. In the case of the former the differences are, perhaps, less marked than with the latter. Leslie Weatherhead, both at Brunswick Chapel, Leeds, and as minister of the City Temple, a man of note in many fields, has himself exercised so distinctive a ministry as to stand apart. In his day he drew a great following and was of service to many, both in the pulpit and in the privacies of personal counsel, where his extensive knowledge of psychology was of the utmost value.

But with Sangster the case is different. Here was a man who seemed to combine within himself, to a rare degree, most of the characteristics common to, and indeed expected of, the eminent Wesleyan Methodist minister standing in a tradition stemming perhaps more from the prosperous years of 'establishment'

Methodism than from its earlier, almost revolutionary, beginnings in a distant day. His ministry belongs to the period chiefly before, during, and after the Second World War. At the Central Hall, Westminster, where he succeeded the celebrated Dinsdale Young, he had a notable and great ministry. When the Central Hall was a refuge for thousands during the bombing, it was heroic. At the same time, it seemed, at any rate to the observer from outside, to include that element of the histrionic sometimes noticeable in those who have given primacy of place in their ministries to the Word. Here was a man, in fact, who combined with other gifts that of being a virtuoso of the pulpit. Crowds pressed to hear him. But it is difficult to imagine him upon Tower Hill. Rather would the natural setting of such a ministry seem to be one of those great buildings of Wesleyan Methodism put up, often at the turn of the century, when the tradition was in its heyday. The pulpit, large and gleaming, was prominent. Acres of seating confronted it, galleries surrounded it, and organ and choir behind gave promise of ample musical accompaniment. Out of sight, in the minister's study at home, was the intellectual discipline which, in theory at any rate, was an essential accompaniment to so high a view of the preaching ministry. Sangster himself wrote of it: 'The man who jealously guards his morning hours for deep study, and study which centres in God's Book; who lets it be known to his people that, while he is available at any hour of the day or night for the dying (and other needs which brook no delay) he expects to be left undisturbed in his pulpit preparation until lunch-time; who uses these fenced hours first for praying, then for brooding on the Bible and for the flinty kind of thinking which will enable him to go twice a Sunday to his pulpit and really feed his people from the Word of God . . . that man will not lack his reward.'[1]

It is impossible to fit Donald Soper into such a setting. Where then, in his own tradition, is he to be placed? Among the scholars, perhaps; men such as Luke Wiseman, Alexander

[1] Paul Sangster, *Dr Sangster* (Epworth Press, 1962).

Findlay, W. F. Moulton, A. S. Peake, Leslie Mitton and many another? Hardly: Soper would be the last to claim any distinction of that nature. Nor has he ever been a Methodist statesman deeply involved in the politics of his own Church. Nor has he appeared much upon the world's scene of the ecumenical movement, which is a pity, for he would have had much to give. This was certainly the opinion of Eric Baker. 'It has always been one of my great regrets that Donald has never played any part in the wider ecumenical movement. This might have happened if a most unfortunate occurrence had not taken place in 1954. He was appointed by the Methodist Church as one of its representatives to the Second Assembly of the World Council of Churches at Evanston, Illinois. He arrived just before the Council was due to begin, and then received an urgent message from his mother to say that his father was dangerously ill. I have often wondered what might have happened had he remained there, and had he made an impact upon that Council. It would have been a volcanic sort of impact. It would not have been universally acceptable, and yet it would have been something they had to consider and at times they would not have been able to ignore. He would then have become a world Christian personality in a way that has never happened. It is not, I think, an exaggeration to suppose that the whole course of the ecumenical movement might have been something in which he had played a big part.'

It is true that Soper has travelled much, though with markedly different degrees of acceptability in different places. He would be unlikely to be *persona grata* in South Africa. Nor is it likely that his political opinions would commend themselves to all Americans, no more, for that matter, than they do to his own countrymen. But he had a wonderful reception when, together with the theologian, the late Paul Tillich, he gave the Earle Lectures at Berkeley, California. In Australia he incurred a public rebuke from the Prime Minister of that country. He has transplanted Tower Hill to Ceylon, among other places, and answered crowd questions there in the same manner. He could hardly be described, none the less, as an ambassador for his Church, in the manner of so many Christian notables of modern times, suffering torture by a thousand handshakes in the process of building bridges of goodwill.

Could it be, then, that Soper's place within his own tradition is to be found in that strain of political radicalism which was a marked feature of early Methodism? British Socialism, said a one-time Secretary of the Labour Party, Morgan Phillips, was not Marxist but Methodist. The statement may well no longer apply, as all politics have tended to become based less upon matters of principle and more upon opportunism. But it was not always so. One of the founders of Chartism, John Rayner Stephens, was a Wesleyan Methodist minister. Joseph Arch, pioneer of agricultural trade unionism, was a Primitive Methodist. So was Peter Lee of the Miners' Association, as it was then called, who has given his name to a town in County Durham. The word 'chapel', for that matter, has long been a part of the vocabulary of trade unions. Soper, as one of the keepers of the conscience of British socialism, and therefore as one of its fiercest critics from time to time, is certainly within this tradition.

But there remains still a great deal of him outside any of these categories. None of them, for instance, bears witness to his essential spirituality. It may well be, therefore, that to place him fully in context it is necessary to go back far beyond any of these particular manifestations of Methodism, and to see in him represented, albeit in modern dress, some of those qualities of the movement which it has had from the beginning. What are they? They have been summarised admirably by Rupert E. Davies in his book on Methodism. After pointing out that Methodism is 'a recurrent form of Christianity', a form of protest against anything, especially institutional form and authority, which tends to interpose itself between the ordinary man and the free access of his soul to God, he goes on to say: 'If we take eighteenth-century Methodism as the norm, the dominant characteristics of this form of Christianity are at once clear, and can be simply set down. The first is a complete and whole-hearted acceptance of the cardinal doctrines of the Christian faith, as conveniently laid down in the historic creeds, combined with the conviction that doctrine which is not proved in devotion and life, and does not issue in practical charity, is valueless; in the last resort, "experimental religion" (as John Wesley called it) is greatly preferable to doctrinal orthodoxy, if the choice has to be made between them. The second is insistence that the heart of Christianity lies in the personal commerce of a man with his Lord, who has saved him and won the forgiveness of his sins, and will live in him to transform his character. The third is stress on the doctrine of the Holy Spirit, the Person of the Trinity, who is often neglected by institutional Christianity, yet without whom neither the fulfilment of the Lord's commandments, nor the common life of the Christian community, is more than a vague aspiration. The fourth is the earnest and patient attempt to embody the "life in Christ", of which the New Testament speaks, in personal and social "holiness", and the formation for this purpose of small groups of committed people who will encourage, correct, instruct, edify and support each other. The fifth is the desire to make known the Gospel, and above everything else the love and pity of God for each individual sinner, on the widest possible scale and in the most persuasive possible terms. The sixth is a generous concern for the material as well as for the spiritual welfare of the under-privileged. The seventh is the development of a Church Order in which the laity stands alongside the minister, with different but equally essential functions, sharing with the ministry the tasks of preaching the Gospel, caring for the Christian flock, and administering the Church's affairs.'[1]

No one, and certainly not Soper, would, or could, claim in himself to measure up to so severe a standard. But we are not attempting to measure his achievements so much as to discover some framework within which he can be placed. And if it is

[1] Rupert E. Davies, *Methodism* (Penguin Books, 1963).

accepted that it is truly here that he belongs, as the modern exponent of a form of Christian protest as old as the hills, of a form of Christianity constantly striving to reach back to those qualities so clearly discoverable in the earlier centuries, then a significant fact emerges. It is that, even if unconsciously, Donald Soper may be representative of perhaps the one form of Christianity which is likely to survive in a world in which it sometimes seems inevitable that the institutional Church of any kind, as it has developed over the ages, must become obsolescent. It is already, and on a world scale, showing signs of doing so as human life and man's power over it, leave less and less room for an institutional God. It is here, then, that the importance of such a witness as Soper's may really reside. He is, and has long been, the proponent of a Christianity which can exist in its own right and in a form which it has taken from the beginning; a minority movement for those few in any age who have felt moved by the spirit to seek God, and to serve him and, in his name, to venture out into the world.

Soper's life, to date, has spanned one of the most troubled and extraordinary epochs of human affairs. All sorts and conditions of men and events are to be encountered in the narrative of it. But it is a story of difficulties rather than of triumphs; of battles rather than of victories. It is therefore much in character that Soper, preaching in Kingsway Hall some years ago took, for a series of five addresses, some of the verses of Faber's hymn 'It is Hard to Work for God' which the Methodist hymn book omits. One of the verses was this:

> Oh it is hard to work for God
> To rise and take His part
> Upon this battlefield of earth,
> And not sometimes lose heart.

But his story, like all those that are worth telling, must begin at the beginning.

## 2

# The Makings of the Man

> One morning, when I was thirteen years of age, I came down to breakfast and the question arose as to what I was going to be. My father said, with all the deep conviction that he had, that he would like his son to be a minister. You would have had to know my father to appreciate that that was neither pompous nor cant: it was what he meant. I remember my reaction, I said 'O.K., I will.'
>
> D.O.S. speaking on the BBC's 'Five to Ten' programme, January 1969

IN KING EDWARD'S far off times, in middle-class families, everyone seemed to be learning the piano. It was a good time for home-made music, and the sounds of it could be heard, on many an evening, here and there across suburbia, coming from windows lit by the intimate glow of gas. The more culturally ambitious the family the more copious, as a general rule, the music. And in those where plain living and high thinking was the rule, music was the permitted indulgence. 'In the days of my youth', wrote W. R. Matthews, for many years Dean of St Paul's, 'nearly everyone seemed to be learning to play the piano, or was at least ready, on very slight provocation, to stand up and sing a solo.'[1]

That was in Camberwell. Some years later, and not far away, in Wandsworth, another family of the same sort, intelligent, purposeful, and religious, was also making music. These were the Sopers, of Knoll Road, Wandsworth.

'My parents', Matthews wrote, 'were "God-fearing" in the evangelical mode and were prominent members of the church

[1] W. R. Matthews, *Memories and Meanings* (Hodder & Stoughton, 1969).

where I was christened. This meant that they were concerned about sin and salvation.' Exactly the same thing could have been said about the Sopers. In fact it was said. 'My life was church-centred in an almost complete sense', Donald Soper recalled years later. 'My father was dedicated to the Church as well as to the faith of which the Church is representative, and my mother also.' The difference, much sharper then than now, was that the Matthews were Anglican, the Sopers, Wesleyan Methodist. Their musical enthusiasms, however, were undenominational, and serve as identification marks of type and background in both cases. With the Sopers, at least, musical enthusiasms persisted. In the early twenties, by which time there were three children, Donald, his younger brother Meredith Ross, known to the family as Sos, and sister Millicent, were still busy with them. The whole family would give concerts, or, at home in the evenings, the two boys would play together; Donald at the piano, Sos the violin, the father singing bass, the mother contralto, Millicent soprano. The Donald Soper who, years later, noted of one of his critics on Tower Hill that he 'could pick out *Love's Old Sweet Song* on a piano, with enthusiasm and a stabilised bass note', may here be seen emerging.

Musically, and in appearance for that matter, the Sopers were striking people and the impression which this close family circle could make upon a visitor was considerable. Eric Baker long afterwards remembered visiting them. 'They were all very beautiful. The family, as a family, could sustain a complete musical evening. I have sat for long periods, listening to Donald and Sos accompanying each other, not playing any set music at all, but knowing what each other was going to do and playing together. There was a very close rapport between them.'

It was a circle soon to be broken. Sos, so called because his sister, as a child, could not pronounce the 'R' in his second name, died as a young man. The event has a lasting significance to the story of his elder brother. The two had been singularly close: great friends, both good athletes, linked, it would seem, by something comparable to that bond which, although they were not twins, unites some twins. Suddenly, on a day in the twenties, Sos was gone. In the opinion of two close observers of Donald Soper, the event marked the end of the only real friendship he was ever to have. A man of multitudinous acquaintances, he has yet been, on the whole, one who has found it difficult to find relationships outside his own family circle, on a personally more intimate level. If this is so, perhaps the death of Sos might have had something to do with it. It is certainly the case that, more than forty-five years later, he spoke of the death of his brother as 'the greatest sorrow of my life. So long ago; but it still seems as if it were yesterday. . . .'

Ernest Frankham Soper, the father of this family, was an average adjuster in the City of London, an employment which his son once described as 'a very erudite and almost exotic occupation which I never really understood'. That is not surprising, since an average adjuster, then as now, is involved with recondite matters of marine insurance. What they were, and how he dealt with them, however, were no part of the domestic life of Ernest Soper. But his employment was reflected in his intelligence. He was an able man, a notable linguist, as his work required. He was also a person of impregnable convictions; convictions which he was in the habit of defending on a narrow front all his life: God, Wesleyan Methodism, and a teetotalism so absolute as to be elevated to the level of a sacred cause. He was very active in this cause. His son remembered that part of his father's equipment which, as a lecturer on the evils of drink he needed to take with him, was a collection of dummy bottles labelled with the names of the various alcoholic liquids which were to be condemned. Abhorrence of alcohol was not, of course, unusual in a man of Ernest Soper's religious outlook. But his teetotalism may well have been intensified by the fact that drink had played a disastrous part in his own family history, and that he had had, by his own strength of character, to rise clear of the wreckage of it. And, like many converts—and he was one—he held to what he regarded as the saving truths which he had received with marked tenacity. His son inherited this convinced teetotalism and maintained it through a far more sophisticated and wide-ranging life than his father ever knew. This father remained the same to the end, 'a man of steadfast faith and high principles which he never made any attempt to hide', as the *Methodist Recorder* said of him in the May of 1962, when he died in his ninety-second year.

This Ernest Frankham Soper, then, when he set out each morning from Knoll Road, Wandsworth, in those early days of the century, to his work in the City, could have been seen as a tall, very thin, handsome man with an auburn moustache and blue eyes. And each day, when he left the house, so also did his wife, Caroline Amelia; a small, intense schoolmistress with the same steel core of principle at the centre of her character as had her husband. Two things at least they had in common, these two; these earnest parents 'who did for their children's good conspire'; an ardent Christian faith expressed through Wesleyan Methodism, and that abhorrence of alcohol which in her case, as well as in his, had been reinforced by personal family misforturnes. Of these parents, and of the home they made, their son Donald said: 'My father stood in a very particular relationship to me from my earliest age, because he was not only my father at home; he was also my Sunday school superintendent at church. I can't say that in those early days I had a warm, easy affection for him. I had a really healthy respect for him and I belonged to him, but he was a very austere man and had great difficulties in his own family life to overcome. In fact, he had to look after a great many members of his family. He was a Roman parent in the very strict sense of that word. And I must confess that my impression was quite often that he was not particularly pleased with me. He hoped for better things.

'My mother was very busy and was often very tired. She was a schoolteacher and a very competent one, under the old London Teachers' Association. She was a most militant person. She stood about four foot eleven and had all the qualities of a suffragette, and all the militancy of those who were not going to be put upon by the male sex. She was deeply devoted to my father and in many respects seemed to me to obey him rather than be conjoined with him in corporate effort. With my brother and my sister we were a particularly close-knit family. But there were two other persons in it. One was Aunt Liza, or Lizzie, who was bridesmaid at my mother's wedding and who, the year after, came and acted as a kind of manageress of our affairs because my mother, naturally, was out at work and father was in the City. Another person called Aunt Nellie, who was a fellow teacher with my mother, also lived with us. Aunt Nellie and Aunt Lizzie were almost as in close propinquity with our affairs as my father and mother themselves were. My father lived a very disciplined life. He was a very strict teetotaller, as I still am. He was a non-smoker. He looked askance at anything which smacked of the theatre. In fact I didn't go to a theatre until I was twenty-one. Our Sundays were of the most rigorous type. We were allowed only "Sunday literature" and we went to church almost unremittingly, our only final escape being when father said it was a good thing to go to bed early on Sunday. If we'd stayed up we should have still been committed to further ecclesiastical exercises, and we were played out. However, I never resented this because of one simple fact, which I think is worth recalling, and that is that it meant everything to my father. There was no scintilla of hypocrisy or half-heartedness about him: he was so completely and absolutely committed to Christianity.'

Donald's own earliest memory was of being, when very young, in a London hospital with scarlet fever and of having, as a reward for staunch conduct, a musical top presented to him with which he was allowed to play in the ward. But the great moment, the great memory was of getting home again, to see his mother waving a welcome at what was the secure centre of the world, 36 Knoll Road, Wandsworth. Everything happened there. Relatives were near by, including a grandfather who had been, incidentally, one of the original trio in a once-celebrated book, Jerome K. Jerome's *Three Men in a Boat*. But what also happened at this Soper home in Knoll Road, Wandsworth, and Streatham and Forest Hill, to both of which places the family moved in the course of the years, was so perfectly representative of the nonconformist, Puritan tradition, once a very powerful element in English society, as to merit, for at least two reasons, a closer look. In the first place, it has now vanished so utterly as to have the attraction of a curiosity. In the second, since it not uncommonly led to powerful reactions when they came to adult life from those who grew up in it, this life style of Donald Soper's parents is relevant to the matter of his own development.

It was a *modus vivendi* based upon the proposition that life was a very serious matter indeed, carrying with it an ultimate accountability to God for the use made of time and talents. Every moment of it had, as far as was possible, to be usefully employed, and this principle extended into the area of recreation as well as that of work. One worked hard; one played hard; and it was necessary to strive in both, if not to excel, at any rate to make the attempt. Life was real; life was earnest. It was also full of duties, abounding in obligations, especially that of frequently, and at times embarrassingly publicly, acknowledging the supremacy of that righteous God under whose eye lived, whether they were aware of it or not, all creatures that on earth did dwell. One of the trials of an otherwise extremely happy childhood which Millicent Lawrence, Donald's sister, remembered, was of having to endure the curious glances of other diners when, in a restaurant, her father insisted on saying grace as at home, loud and long, in the same manner as that in which he took daily family prayers.

It was part of this pattern of early endeavour that, when the family went on holdiay, the emphasis was on vigorous activity. The ideological basis of this lay no doubt in the conviction that sloth was wicked, and thus to be avoided. The application of the principle, however, could be exhausting. Thus all holiday time, for the Sopers, was planned by their father, with a view to pressing in as much activity as possible into the time available, it being naturally assumed that this would bring the maximum benefit to all concerned. There was no time for sitting on the beach. Vigorous bathing was obligatory, followed by tennis and a long walk. If time permitted—and it could be made to permit if the walks were rapid enough—there would be time for another bathe. After that, as like as not, there would be cricket on the sands, possible followed by yet another walk. The two boys, at least, enjoyed this regimen vastly: their father was an excellent athlete, and so were they. Sundays, of course, were already planned. One of the first acts of Soper senior, on arriving at whatever bracing resort had been chosen for the family stay, was to ascertain the locality of the nearest Wesleyan Methodist church. It was a matter of course that all should attend, as at home, morning and evening. At home they also attended afternoon Sunday school. Both parents were in the church choir and Ernest Soper was, in addition to being superintendent of the Sunday school, superintendent of the Band of Hope.

Both parents, ardent supporters of this way of life, need to be seen as people rather than types. They were not types; but highly individual persons, and both physically handsome. At the same time, both had a severe look, until age mellowed them. Millicent Lawrence recalled them: 'Father was a very stern man; very just, puritanical in outlook and, we thought, as children, sometimes rather lacking in mercy or kindness. There was no grey with him; everything was either black or white. Black was anything that he considered wrong. We weren't allowed to go to theatres. We were allowed to go to cinemas, occasionally, but not to dances when we were young, although as we got older we were. Mother was of a much softer nature, but she was very dominated by father. What he said, we had to do. I think he had a sense of humour; but it was a controlled one, and the little things of life which were, to us, very funny he didn't see. I think his thoughts were on much higher things.'

These two, then, with all that they stood for, profoundly

influenced the development of Donald Soper. Indeed, they continued to observe him, during his public life, with a pride which none the less never excluded criticism. His mother, indeed, when her son entered the House of Lords, held it necessary to remind him, as though honours, being vanities, could be a pitfall, that he was still a Methodist minister and neither more, nor less.

The family life they created, given such a picture as this, could easily enough cause a smile. But the smile would be misplaced. These were able people; they produced able people, and it may be allowed that the disappearance of the principle-based life style they followed has left a gap in society yet to be filled. But, most importantly, they produced a happy home. Restriction did not create gloom, even if it sometimes made for friction, as when Donald, who loved dancing, wanted to go to dances and did. The family life of these Sopers, in fact, was markedly gay. Millicent Lawrence remembered: 'Every evening when they were home together, when they grew up, the two boys would sit down. Donald would play the piano, Sos the violin. They would go on playing tunes until just before bed. And often the three of us (I used to sing, too) would do Negro spirituals and Donald would give a talk about them, and we would illustrate them.'

Even so, happy as this family life may have been, it was one from which, in the usual course of events, some members of it might have been expected to rebel as soon as they were able. Literature and public life alike provide many instances of sons who have reacted against strong fathers, especially when religious disciplines were part of the strength. Thus Samuel Butler might not have followed the way of all flesh quite so depressingly if his grandfather had not been a bishop and his father a canon. Hugh Dalton might not have been so aggressive, and even, to some of his colleagues, detestable as a Socialist politician, if his father had not been a rather odd, if not to say objectionable, Canon of Windsor. But with Donald Soper there is no trace of this reaction to be found—a surprising fact in view of his marked strength and independence of character. This could be a tribute to the shining goodness of his father, who may well have succeeded in the difficult task of making something attractive of virtue practised on a narrow front. The true explanation, however, seems to lie elsewhere. It emerged in a radio interview with the writer and broadcaster, Norman St John Stevas who, talking with Donald Soper, asked him, 'Did you ever feel any desire to rebel, in your home?' The reply was; 'I never felt the slightest desire to rebel against, shall we say, the exercises of the Christian Church. I'd rebelled against its principles, and if I've given anybody the idea that any of the saintliness of my parents rubbed off on me, let me eradicate that straight away. I wasn't a very reputable boy—I say it quite sincerely—but what is true, and this is a very interesting reflection, that I liked the things that belonged to the Church. Unlike some people, I did not want to stay away from the Church at the first opportunity I had. I loved being there. I can remember the first Sunday I was free not to go to church. I was a bayonet-fighting instructor in the Cadet Corps, teaching men old enough to be my father to stick bayonets into one another, down in Devonshire. I was in the Sergeants' Mess, in a tent with some other men, and I was just a boy of fifteen. It was Sunday morning, and I ran four miles to church, not because I was good but because that was where I wanted to be. It may sound almost like cant, but I never rebelled against the Church because that was where I found happiness, even as a child.'

This absorption in the Church as represented by, and indeed confined to, the community of the local Methodist body, was total. But, as Donald indicated in the interview, such absorption should not in any sense be misconstrued as a mark of piety. It was just that the local church gave a vigorous and high-spirited boy all that he wanted in the way of fun and games and girls—the latter especially of much fascination for Donald. He was not, at this stage of his life, in any way a thinker. That came later. But he did seek pleasures; music, considerable flirtations, and that personal popularity which always came easily his way. The Church provided all. Anyone with first-hand knowledge of a lively Methodist church of even thirty years ago can understand how easily this could happen. The plain building, often with pitch-pine pews and dominant organ, would be the centre of a whole complex of activities, secular and sacred, which could easily absorb the whole of life in a highly satisfactory manner. This may well be no longer the case; but the assumption that society has in general gained from this loss should be resisted. The plain fact was that, for Donald Soper, as no doubt for others like him in those simpler days, Church was fun as well as deeper things.

There was, even so, a weakness in the situation in that it tended to be so all-absorbing as to be over-exclusive. In later years, especially in radio interviews, when Lord Soper of Kingsway had become a notable figure, he would be sometimes asked what, in the days of his youth, when he had been so obviously and exclusively Methodist, has been his attitude towards lesser breeds without the law, such as Anglicans and Roman Catholics. His answer, as the scripts bear witness, is that he scarcely knew any, so entirely was his world that of his own communion. It needed an incident, in his later teens, to bring the fact home to him, that other kinds of people with other kinds of convictions, existed. 'If you are brought up in an environment which is so exclusively religious, you don't really meet other sorts of people at all. So I can't remember any cogent or collected thoughts about those "outside". I do remember very distinctly, on the first Armistice Day, there was at school the son of a local Communist who refused to stand still at the silence and walked round the playground. I was captain of the school, and I remember I knew I had to defend this youngster from the attacks that were made upon him for this. Afterwards, I wondered why I had defended him. I knew, I suppose, it was my job and I think, if it isn't pompous to say so, that it was at that stage that I began to entertain thoughts about those who were in a very different frame of mind to my own; that people believed in quite different things to the ones that I believed in. And I think I learned a certain amount of tolerance.'[1]

The incident, significant as to the later development of Soper as a life-long defender of minorities, has an importance also in saying something about the historical background to his youth. It was a grim background. Born in 1903, the boy was eleven in 1914. If Donald had been born a few years earlier, it is more than possible that he would have died in Flanders. As it was, the nearest this ultimately life-long pacifist came to martial exercise was to be sergeant-major of his school Cadet Corps; and a bayonet instructor who ran those morning miles from camp to church. But the First World War was the sombre background of much of his boyhood, and the undertone to those Soper musical evenings was, for five years at least, the sound of the guns. What happened when it was all over at last we cannot know. Perhaps Ernest Soper did something surprising, like the father of Malcolm Muggeridge in Croydon, who came home and, in temporary contradiction of his political principles, displayed a Union Jack from a bedroom window. But the long-term effect of growing up in wartime, and in the sour and disastrous aftermath of the twenties, was obviously of much importance to the eventual emergence of Donald Soper as pacifist and Socialist.

Meanwhile he was sent to Aske's School, Hatcham, where he appeared to succeed in everything with that facility which could have been a danger to him in later life, had a craggy conscience, combined with often unpopular principles, not intervened. But at school, before the days of conscience and principles, he does seem to have been the golden boy, to some rather irritatingly so. His sister, for example, could never understand why, although he rarely appeared to do any work, he usually passed all his examinations. He would read; but as she and Sos plodded through their homework night after night,

[1] BBC programme 'Frankly Speaking' (29.7.65).

Donald seemed uninvolved. Her theory was that he did it all in the train, being aided by that phenomenal memory—described later by one of his Cambridge tutors as 'a blotting-paper memory'—which many noticed in him later on. He was a very handsome boy: outspoken, prepared to speak to anybody on anything. He also spoke very well. People would turn, on social occasions when the Sopers were present, to see who was this boy with the brilliant conversation. He was also arrogant, and his sister, understandably, was indignant of his superiority. But his father looked upon him with restrained pride, seeing him destined for the highest honour which that God-fearing man could conceive—the ministry. Thus it came about that, when Donald was thirteen, his father told him of his wish and the boy agreed. The matter, however, was to prove more complicated than either foresaw at that time. All in all, there is something excessive about the Donald Soper of these early days. He was good at everything, games included, indeed, games especially. This, on one occasion, led to tragedy. He was a very fast bowler, and during a school match, he had the misfortune to kill the batsman when the ball rose and hit the boy over the heart. The degree to which this upset Donald at the time, and the persistence of the memory of it—he was recalling it fifty years later—suggest an abhorrence of violence which was possibly an unconscious ingredient of his later pacifism.

This was in the summer of 1921, when Donald was in the last term of a highly successful, completely conformist, school career. In the autumn of the same year he went up to Cambridge on an Exhibition to St Catharine's. There, as suddenly and as predictably, the secure world in which he had grown up a virtually unchallenged success, fell apart. He had never before been away from home: had never known anything but discipline and order on the one hand, and the close fellowship of the Church on the other. And now, on the same kind of October evening as many freshmen have known, with the lights coming on over Cambridge, and strangers everywhere, this young man, not nearly so confident or so competent as he appeared, found himself abruptly possessed of the large and adult freedom of the university.

He was given a room out of college; a landlady who had seen many like him before, and a tutor who merely asked to see him further in a few days time. He was of no importance, and appeared to have nothing very pressing, certainly nothing organised, to do. He was also, as it happened, unwell, suffering with painful boils on chin and neck together with an internal displacement described to him, in the terminology of the time, as a floating kidney. In spite of enormous vitality, now and later, he was not, as it happened, at any time a fully fit man, and pain and discomfort of some sort or other was to be his lot throughout life. For the moment, the chief effect was that he was prevented from playing games. He had never, all in all, been quite as miserable in his life as the first part of that first Cambridge term. He had been, possibly, too successful too easily and too early; and the combination, as not infrequently happens, had proved an inadequate preparation for life. Such acute depressive periods in young people, better understood now than then, can be dangerous. One night, driven by the pain he was enduring from one of his boils, he took his razor blade in the dark and with it cut off part of his chin.

But the blackness passed quite soon. Not for the first time, his musical virtuosity brought the sunshine out again. There was a freshers' concert at which he was a brilliant success. He played the piano and was enthusiastically received. The Captain of Boats invited him to tea the next day, and he had arrived.

But all that, of course, was superficial, as the events of the first term usually are. On a far deeper level Donald Soper's five years at Cambridge were to be of critical and lasting importance. It was the time when most of the decisions were made which determined the basic attitudes for the rest of his life. It was a time of revolutionary change in his growing up into manhood: it was a time of comprehensive change in both his religious and political

. The Soper the world has since known was thus to a larg... xtent formed, not by that God-fearing, earnest home in Wandsworth, Streatham and Forest Hill but by the university of Cambridge.

There was, none the less, one incident during his first year which sprang from the background of his childhood and yet, being brought about by the wider horizons of Cambridge, may be seen as a link, like the little Bridge of Sighs crossing the Cam in St John's between two worlds. He became temporarily an atheist. The experience was important to his development at the time and also subsequently. His own description of it came in a radio programme many years later. 'I went up as a member of the Church, coming out of a beautiful and good home. I assumed that Christianity was true because it was so obviously true for my father, it was so obviously true for my mother, and, what was more important, it was so obviously the kind of life which had given me happiness. I had no desire to move away from the Church because it was the Church where I had made friends. Therefore for me religion was as natural as eating and sleeping. And then an angel in disguise—although it was a very good disguise at the time—persuaded me to read Lecky's *History of Rationalism*. At the end of it I was a confessed and complete atheist, which I found most disturbing. The position was complicated because I promised my father that I would go to church and, if required, be a Sunday school teacher.

'I went to the Sunday school superintendent, a very knowledgable man, and I put my case before him. He saw the point at once. He said, "My boy, when you get your faith back, come and see me again." I was much gratified when he went on to say, "Now, what can we do?" I said that obviously I could not take a Sunday school class, but would he allow me to be the Sunday school pianist? I could play the hymns in secular fashion, but I could still be within the framework of the Church, which was where I wanted to be. And so, all the time I was an atheist, which wasn't very long, I was a Sunday school pianist on these terms. I think that this was good for me because I found the environment of the church was such that I realised what I was throwing away, as well as the intellectual problems that were facing me. Gradually these took shape, and I had some long talks with some knowledgeable people. Gradually I came back, not to the uncritical faith which I had held before; but at least to a modicum of the faith, and I never lost it.'

Asked what it was exactly the book did to him, he said: 'It was the dubiety that it first engendered about the actual basic belief of the Christian; the existence of God, the divinity of Jesus Christ, the credibility of the New Testament, and of the Christian Church. All these things had been accepted by me, as I have said, as if they were self-evident truths. It was the corrosive effect of being compelled to ask the questions as to whether in fact it was true which had this devastating effect on me. I hadn't been trained—and I think this is a criticism of the way I had been brought up—on Christian evidence with anything like the care which I've been compelled to foster, for instance, in talking about it in the open air ever since. What happened was—and I think it's happening now and I think it's of general significance—that I was no longer sure that the things which were set out as dogmatic truths were, in fact, true. I came to the point that they were not true for me. The kind of faith to which I returned has never been as dogmatic and has never been as comprehensive, or as self-evident to me as the one I lost. In fact, I am a Christian agnostic in many things today, and I've learned that the idea of Christianity as something which provides the answers to any question which can conceivably be asked is sheer nonsense. I have to live on the iron rations of a number of simple truths which I really do believe, and as regards a great deal of the other material which I might once upon a time have accepted, I leave that.

'This was the great change that took place and it has characterised my own thinking ever since. But it was quite revolutionary and quite dramatic at the time, and I think, to make a comment on it, that the idea that reigned until the nineteenth century that Christianity was a series of self-evident truths is a fallacy. I was much comforted, on going back, to the New Testament, to find how little of this there is in the teaching of Jesus. . . . I am sure of a dictum which I learned from my philosophy tutor at Cambridge, that all religion presupposes natural religion, and that you have no right to accept anything for the good of your soul unless it has the appearance of reason. We are not, in fact, in two worlds; but in one. And what is intellectually insufferable can never be a consolation, finally, to the human spirit. It was only when I was confronted with these intellectual backgrounds to it, which had never come to me in this form before, that I realised that the background of moral obligation, and of emotional feeling, must be the rationality or the reasonableness of the world in which these things are claimed for the Christain faith.'

The philosphy tutor referred to in this passage was F. R. Tennant, whom Donald encountered at Wesley House, Cambridge. To this then recently opened Methodist theological college he had gone after reading history, to complete the first part of his Tripos at St Catharine's. He read for Part II the Philosophy of Religion. Tennant, who lectured in this subject, was a very considerable scholar and theologian who had a lasting influence upon Donald. The nature of that influence was described by Harold Roberts, a theologian himself, in later years Principal of Richmond College, President of Conference and a leading figure in the Anglican–Methodist Conversations of the sixties. In these early days he was assistant tutor of Wesley House. 'Tennant', he said, 'was a great authority on the doctrine of sin. He was a very lucid lecturer who took the Natural Science Tripos himself when he was an undergraduate, and then switched over to theology. He was very particular about the way he expressed himself, and about the use of words. He used to say that he would like to have outside his lecture room a notice "Eschew ambiguity, those who enter here".' That obviously appealed to Donald very much because, right through his ministry, people have often remarked on his lucidity, on his careful use of words, and I think he would be prepared to admit that he owed some measure of debt to Dr Tennant. Donald was, of course, a great mimic, Tennant had his own vocabulary and, somehow or other, Donald seemed to have no difficulty whatsoever in remembering the rather peculiar and difficult terms which Tennant used to employ. What would have surprised Tennant himself is that sometimes Donald gave them a rather different meaning from that which he had given. But that does not mean to say that he did not know what meaning Tennant had given to them; but that for the benefit of his audience he used to bring the lecture up to date. One finds, when listening to him in the open air, traces of the training he received under Tennant, and he would be the first, I think, to admit that not only in the matter of language, or in lucidity, but also in the content of his theology, he owed a great debt to that great teacher.

'I do not know whether he realised at the time what value this course was to him. But those who listen to him now know how ready he is to give a rational basis to the faith that is in him. He has never succumbed to irrationalism. I think the fact that he was able to lay the foundations of the study of philosophy of religion in his student days accounts, in part, for the facility and the effectiveness with which he has been able to deal with the various intellectual problems that he has encountered.'

In the small, close community of Wesley House—small enough for each of its members to be closely observed—something of the Donald Soper which was to endure through the years became visible. The attractive boy had grown into a very attractive young man: popular with all sorts and conditions of people. Thus already that danger which had been apparent in his boyhood, and which later he had to resist, inherent in the popularity he could so easily arouse, was clearly present. The offence he gave to the conventional in after times, when his unorthodox convictions and identification with minority opinions made him something of an odd man out, may possibly have arisen at this point. He disappointed many would-be admirers because he declined to be what they wished to admire. He could so easily have become that most fatuous of public figures, of whom there has been a long line, originally sired by fervour out of verbosity, the popular evangelist.

At this time, too, there became evident an ability to commend himself and his cause to people with no use for religion whatever. This was to enable him later on to pass through many doors usually closed to his kind. Not a few of his Cambridge friends, indeed, were a little surprised when he entered the ministry. An incident by which he added to this surprise was described by Harold Roberts.

'It was customary for students from Wesley House, if they went out on Sunday to conduct a service, to wear a clerical collar because every student of Wesley House was accepted for the ministry, and the first time Donald wore a clerical collar was quite an occasion. He had to go somewhere in East Anglia and it meant setting out on Saturday night. So he resolved to wear his clerical collar on that Saturday night and to visit his old college. Just before Hall, for the first time wearing a clerical collar, he went along to St Catharine's and walked around the court in order that people might know who he was. It caused a great deal of amusement. But it was characteristic of him nevertheless, although he did it to amuse and not to edify, that he was not ashamed of his profession.'

One curious characteristic likewise emerged at this time—a love of jokemaking whenever opportunity offered. This had been part of his home background, possibly as a reaction to the gravity of Ernest Soper, whose deeply ingrained conviction of the seriousness of life did not easily permit laughter. One result was that there was a great deal of it, as Millicent Soper and others remembered, in the family circle. But now Donald, like a cracker manufacturer determined to pop a joke into every one of his products, extended the practice until it became a habit. Examples of it can be found all over the record of his public utterances. Thus, in a brilliant maiden speech in the House of Lords, half a century after these Cambridge days, he could not resist saying that the existence of the place was 'testimony to the reality of life after death'. Again, remembering how he preached his first sermon in a small church outside Cambridge, he had to add, 'it closed soon afterwards. I can only hope there was no connection between the two events.'

At the Methodist Conference of 1953, when all were awaiting some solemn response from him as newly elected President, he brought a roar of laughter by announcing the latest Test score. Yet again, concerning one of his experiences when speaking on Tower Hill, he wrote, in a book otherwise serious in style and intent, 'There was one very eloquent man who came for many years. He was a Cockney, a sailor, who was talking one day about alcohol, concerning which he was an expert. I said that he ought to sign the pledge. Whereat he retorted, "Didn't Paul say, 'Take a little wine for thy stomach's sake'?" I agreed that Paul did, but suggested that Paul meant "Rub it in". He wouldn't accept that as the answer. So I tried to approach him on another track. I told him how dangerous it was to quote Scripture, and I quoted, with what I hoped to be devastating authority, the words from Proverbs, "Wine is a mocker, strong drink is raging, for at the last it biteth like a serpent and stingeth like an adder." And he said he'd been looking for that sort of stuff for the last ten years.'[1]

It could be called a love of fooling. It could be described as a mark of that outward gaiety often assumed by inwardly sad men: like the painted-on grin on the face of a clown. It is in any event unlikely that a man who for so long was to be so feelingly aware of the sombre side of human life, and who was, moreover, to spend his ministry among manifestations of it, would in fact find life naturally a laughing matter. Another great Christian of this century, Geoffrey Studdert Kennedy, the poet and prophet of the First World War and afterwards, had the same character-

[1] Donald Soper, *The Advocacy of the Gospel* (Hodder & Stoughton, 1961).

istic of outward laughter concealing inner sadness. However, here it was in Donald Soper at Wesley House. Here was the wag. Ardent in the cause in which he had been brought up, he would go off to London sometimes to address a temperance meeting and return apparently as drunk as a lord, as though the temptations had overcome even him. He would have difficulty in finding his college and even more the way to his room, to which he would have to be assisted, persisting in what a contemporary remembered as 'a masterly performance' until the door closed. But he was serious enough about temperance, then as always, seeing in drink a threat to a social order which could, and should at its best, reflect the Kingdom of God.

But no one, in manner or outlook, could have been further from self-righteousness. On the contrary, he would seem to have been a very attractive young man. At Wesley House, as during his schooldays, he gave the impression of devoting little time to work. But there were stresses behind the gaiety and the apparent indolence which were not guessed until they became apparent. Thus Harold Roberts, 'The time came for him to take his final examination. During his last year he suffered from nervous strain and it was necessary for him to be away from college for a little time. Some of us wondered what exactly would happen. But he took his examinations and, to our great delight but rather to our surprise in view of the fact that he had had such a difficult year, he took a First Class. It should be said that this was a great achievement. Of course, he was an excellent examinee. He could arrange his material as it ought to be arranged, and it was a pleasure for an examiner to read what he had written. His handwriting was as lucid as his thought and there's no doubt that he deserved the First. And let it be remembered that it was a very difficult subject, because, when it comes to the philosophy of religion, it is a rare thing for anybody who takes that subject to have done anything in philosophy before he came up to university.'

So there he was, Cambridge behind, a life's work before him.

He was perfectly clear as to what that work was to be: the Methodist ministry. But, as time had passed, the fact had become disturbingly apparent that to attain the Methodist ministry was not quite so easy a matter as he had once supposed. His own account of this odd misapprehension is interesting, although allowance has to be made, when noting it, for the habit of levity mentioned. He said, 'I decided at the age of thirteen that I was going to do a job for the Lord, and that he was very lucky to have me. I had a loud voice. That was my only qualification. And I was fairly good at impromptu speaking. In my innocence or in my arrogance, I rather assumed that the day would come when the President of the Conference would come down to see me at Cambridge and say, "Bless you, here's a dog-collar." I think it was Eric Baker who brought me up against reality. He said, "Have you become a local preacher?" I said, "No". He said, "Well, you've got to become a local preacher first." And so this was the time at Cambridge when the real facts of the ministry began to come home to me, and I realised what a young idiot I'd been. Then I did begin to become agitated and worried as to whether it really was my vocation, athough I never really doubted that I wanted to become a minister.'

What actually happened was recalled by Eric Baker.

'The first thing that any man who intends to enter the Methodist ministry must do is to become a local preacher, and Donald began towards that goal quite early in his Cambridge career. I was privileged to accompany him to the first service that he conducted, which was at a little village called Quy, on the Newmarket road from Cambridge. It is said that more Methodist ministers have preached their first sermon at Quy than at any other particular church. The congregation was a very small one, and when a man first began to preach it was natural that the earliest appointment he should receive would be at this tiny place. I played the harmonium for him on that occasion, there being no one else to do it, and I remember that, though the congregation was so small, he had chosen the most elaborate hymns, such as *Sometimes a light surprises*. I can't remember anything about the sermon except that the text was "What lack I yet?"'

What indeed? He was soon to discover the answer when, in the September of 1926, he went as a probationer to the South London Mission.

3

# The Minister

My first sermon lasted twelve and a half minutes, and the farmer who heard it said I had a good singing voice.

D.O.S. in *British Weekly* (15.5.52)

During his examination, when entering the ministry, he had been asked whether he had a passion for souls. He was not aware, he confessed, of having a passion for souls. He was not quite sure what a soul was. But he had a great love for people.

*Sydenham Gazette* (19.2.37)

ONE MONDAY afternoon in the September of 1926, a man in Rivet Street, off the Old Kent Road, announced to his cowering family that he was about to cut his throat. At the same hour, the new probationer to the South London Mission, Oakley Place, opposite Rivet Street, between the Dun Cow and the Duke of Wellington pubs, was about to preside at the Women's Meeting. The Deaconess, informed of the matter, hurried to fetch him. 'When I got there', he remembered, 'he was standing in the middle of the room, drunk, and brandishing his razor. There were one or two children in various corners of the room. I offered to shake hands with him and luckily he put the razor down to shake hands with me, and then one of the kids nipped off with the razor and was two streets away before he could say "Knife".'

That was fortunate: but it was also revealing of at least one of the answers posed by the text of that first student sermon of Donald's, 'What lack I yet?' He lacked social awareness. Places like Rivet Street came to him like a revelation of horrors hitherto unimagined. He said: 'I had lived a sheltered life, in the sense that during the formative years from fifteen to eighteen, I'd been cooped up in London because of the war, and Cambridge was not a particularly expansive kind of education in social conditions. So when I went to the South London Mission straight from Cambridge, I was in fact academically aware of what words like poverty and deprivation and poor housing meant, but to see these things was a profound shock.'

It was, of course, a singularly bleak time in which to enter the working world. A good deal of it was, in fact, not working at all. These were the times of the dole queues; of growing bitterness in the coalfields, and of desperation in the industrial wastelands of the north. Nineteen twenty-six was more than the year of the General Strike (an episode in which Donald, a few months before going to the South London Mission, had found himself, as one who supported the strikers, in a minority position among his student contemporaries). It was also a year among many of the economic depression which lasted, off and on, from the end of the brief boom which followed the First World War to the rearmament scramble immediately presaging the Second. All this time afterwards it can come as a surprise to know that, from the early twenties until 1939, there were never less than a million out of work.

Such facts are of the first importance in any attempt to look at the life and actions of any man who lived, in whatever capacity, through the twenties and thirties. Economic insecurity was a continuing condition; it affected everyone in some way or another. It could make the better-off feel guilty, afraid, indignant or defensive, according to type. It made the poor angry or resigned, again according to type. And it certainly opened the eyes of many including Donald Soper, to some of the realities of existence, and stirred them to seek for the causes and to search for the cure, if such was to be found, of that widely diffused poverty which had, in fact, been an aspect of society from the Industrial Revolution onwards.

That Donald was so astonished by the poverty of South London in 1926 is in itself both a surprising fact and a comment on the religious and social climate of the times. He had lived throughout his childhood, after all, but a few miles away from the outward and visible signs of the poverty which struck him as so extraordinary in the Old Kent Road. No continent separated Knoll Road, Wandsworth, where the godly Sopers held their musical evenings in the days of his youth, from Rivet Street, where the ungodly got drunk when they had the money and fought among themselves. But an enormous social gap lay between. The religious comment arises from the fact that it was not seen as a necessary part of even the most Christian life to try to bridge it. This is not a criticism of the Sopers of Knoll Road: rather is it a comment upon the social structure of a whole society which could, as the middle classes for many generations actually did, live often within sight and sound of poverty and destitution without seriously questioning whether its existence was really necessary. It was true that some did much to try and relieve it: it is equally true that few did much to think of a way past it.

Even in 1933 one observer could note: 'One family I visited lived in an odd little house, consisting of one bedroom, one ground floor room, and a basement kitchen opening into a high-walled yard, and from which almost all light was obscured by surrounding buildings, which pressed right up against it. In these quarters lived a respectable, hard-working man, the kind, hard-working mother and seven children. There had been eight, but the eldest boy had been killed in the war. Father, mother and the two youngest children slept in this room. Three girls slept in the groundfloor room, and the two boys in the kitchen. The mother took in washing.'[1]

This was not a result of the economic depression, as was the case of the man whom a press photograph in the twenties caught in a London street with a board on his back saying. 'I know three trades: I speak three languages, fought for three years, have three children, have no work; but only want one job.' The

[1] Mrs C. S. Peel, *Life's Enchanted Cup* (John Lane, The Bodley Head).

household observed in a basement kitchen was the product of a social system, not of an epoch, and countless like it could have been discovered in any city for generations past. It so happened that the existence of the one stimulated awareness of the other, so that the late twenties and all the thirties were a time of political awakening for many of the intelligentsia. Most of them, thus awakened, went Left, speeded on their way by the menacing rise of Fascism abroad. It was a time of agonised debate. 'A British Radical intelligentsia, comparable to the long-established Continental intelligentsias, did not appear until the 1930s. In the main British intellectuals have always been Liberal or Conservative. Then between 1928 and 1933 a change occurred in their outlook . . . a new seriousness came to the fore in place of the former *joie de vivre*. Increasing attention was given to politics . . . as time passed the politics of the intellectual moved Leftward to Socialism and Communism. What began as a political awakening became a great radicalisation.'[1]

Such, then, was something of the political and social atmosphere of the world in which Donald began his ministry at Oakley Place in the South London Mission. They were important formative years during which he developed and settled into certain convictions regarding his ministry and his politics which were never thereafter greatly to change. The South London Mission and what followed it, the Central London Mission, really saw the makings of the Donald Soper the world later knew. His home had taught him the fundamentals of Christian living; Cambridge had taught him to think about and, in some measure, to criticise them. His first two ministerial appointments taught him many things about applying them to the realities of the world as it was. For the rest of his life, whether as Christian minister, Socialist or pacifist or, as was usually the case, a combination of all three, he can be seen following up and developing these same virtually unchanging convictions.

[1] Neal Wood, *Communism and British Intellectuals* (Gollancz and Columbia University Press, 1959).

Oakley Place, then, taught him a lot. His verdict on his work there, none the less, was adverse. He said: 'I wasn't much good. I found that I was very much out of my element. I hadn't had much training in this sort of thing. I had had a good deal of theological training which did not seem to be much use. But what saved me, in a sense, was that the Church was in a dilapidated condition. I went to the Superintendent, Kedward, and asked whether we could have it redecorated. As there wasn't much money, I thought that we might do it ourselves. I went to a local builder who was also a Methodist and asked him what he would charge and, when he told me, I found it was too much. So, one Sunday evening, I said to the congregation—mainly women—that I proposed to redecorate the church if I could borrow enough of the impedimenta. I also asked them if some of their husbands would come and help. To my astonishment a number of complete strangers turned up. In the end we did the job and had a better congregation afterwards—much better. People may not have been listening to my sermons; they may have been wondering if my sacrilegious hands had been on their paintwork.

'I think, without being sentimental, that this taught me a profound lesson. It was that the moment a church becomes a people's own church, with their handiwork, then it is a different institution. I interpreted my duties not so much in terms of the traditional kind of Bible Study groups and so forth, but much more as creating a centre to which, by all kinds of means, we sought to attract people. I really did get an insight into the sort of life that is commonly called the life of the working classes. I can remember one very moving episode. I noticed one of the healthier-looking members of the congregation, and I remember noticing him limp one day. I asked was the matter and he showed me his leg, ulcerated from knee to ankle. He said his doctor had told him to go to bed. But, if he did go to bed somebody else would take his job, and then where would his money come from? That was burnt into my memory. There was the supreme evil of the Capitalist society, which made people work because otherwise they would starve. It is this terribly disproportionate amount of trouble, or of difficulty, or indeed of suffering that is endured by those who are under the constant threat of insecurity, which struck me.'

But there was another side to this. Within two months of Donald's arrival at Oakley Place as probationer, some of the more orthodox and responsible office bearers agreed that it would be well if he were to be removed at the end of the year. This was not a small matter. Nor is it necessary to assume that all the faults were on one side, and that here was a straight case of the dead hand of convention seeking to restrain originality and enthusiasm. It could be that this young man, undoubtedly brilliant, was also considerably irritating. It could be that here was the beginning of that disapproval of him which not a few in his own communion came to feel, and at times strongly to express, in later times. Then, as later, he was sensitive to it, and sought the advice of his father, who ruled that Donald should tell his Superintendent. This was R. N. Kedward, sometime, in addition to his duties at the South London Mission, Liberal MP for Bermondsey. Donald explained the trouble to him, only to receive the somewhat deflating reply, 'Ah yes, Donald, thank you very much for telling me.' But at the next Quarterly Meeting, when Donald was just about to introduce it with a prayer, the door opened and Kedward came in, announced that he would take the chair, and dealt with the situation so that there was no more trouble.

One of his achievements—neither small nor trivial having regard to the circumstances of time and place—was to stage *The Pirates of Penzance* at Oakley Place. *The Era,* the theatrical paper of the day, commented that this was the best amateur performance that they had seen that year. In the show, of course, there is a mock fight between policemen and pirates. After the dress rehearsal, one or two of the livelier members of the cast suggested that it could be enlivened if a whistle were blown to begin hostilities and another to end them. In between whiles there could be a genuine free-for-all. This was a tremendous success. Each night for a week people came to see the fight. The spiritual benefits of all this would not be easy to define. But pleasure and happiness were given to many people and some sense of fellowship, at least, was created. Even so, Donald, looking back on this, was critical of himself. 'It would be quite false to pretend that in many ways I was a success', he said. 'I was not. I was young and personable to a certain extent. I had the gift of the gab. But it was a very difficult assignment and I have great sympathy with anybody who has that kind of job to do, even today, when the situation is very different.'

It is possible, of course, that the field of action, limited to one particular church, was simply not big enough to engage fully the time and talents he had to offer. If that were so, he was not the only one, then or subsequently, to feel this. There have always been those who have found the ministry as expressed through a localised church too much of a day of small things to satisfy either conscience or predilection, just as there have been those who have found it, apparently, fully absorbing. Whatever the reason in Donald's case, it was during this time that he began, as he put it, 'to spread his wings'. One of the places they carried him to was Tower Hill, but the tale of his open-air ministry there, and elsewhere, must wait. Meanwhile, another extra-mural activity which took his time was reading for his PhD at the London School of Economics. The subject, rather distantly removed from the world of *The Pirates of Penzance* and the Old Kent Road, was Gallicanism and ultra-Montanism. The undertaking was considerable, and the formidable Laski was among the examiners. However, it was in due course accomplished and he received his degree. In 1929, having completed his three years probation, he was ordained and sent to the Central London Mission to be the first minister of a new hall that was to take the place of two traditionally famous Methodist churches—the Liverpool Road Church and the Highbury Church. This was the Islington Central Hall.

He went there as a married man. In his Cambridge days he had met at a party, during some vacation, a schoolgirl of sixteen. This was Marie Dean, one of a family of seven brothers and sisters at that time living in Norbury. She found him, as many did, dominating and attractive. But so was his brother, and for a time she was not sure which to choose of the two. Both, at one time, wanted to be engaged to her. But Donald was chosen in the end, and they were married on 3 August 1929, when she was twenty. They set up house in a small place called Kelross Road, quite near the Islington Central Hall. These two, very different in background—the Deans' church affiliation was indeterminate and she had in fact been to a Roman Catholic school—were destined to live happy ever after. But it was not easy, at least for her, being so young and having to marry not only the man but also, to some degree, the office. But such difficulties, more acute then than now, were at least lessened by the fact that Donald, an extremely self sufficient person, never needed the public help-mate some circles by convention expected. What he did need, and did get, was a home where he could get away from it all and that, in so exposed a public figure, was and remained very precious. But he cannot have been an easy man to get used to, and it says much for his young wife that she adjusted so well to his frequent absences and total absorption in his increasingly wide-ranging work. They were to have four daughters, Ann born in 1931, Bridget two and a half years later; Judith in 1942; Caroline in 1946.

Meanwhile, at Islington, Donald found much to engage him. The seven years there, in his view, 'saw the peak of Central Hall development'. The remark needs some elucidation, both because of an instrinsic interest, and because a Central Hall, either this one at Islington or the one at Kingsway to which, after seven years, Donald was to move, was the framework for the whole of his ministry. Inaugurated by the great Hugh Price Hughes as expressions of the Forward Movement in Wesleyan Methodism at the turn of the century, these places were seen essentially in terms of mission. Thus in 1885 missions were founded in East London and Manchester, in 1886 in Central London, in 1887 in West London, in 1900 in Poplar and Bow. Not churches, but halls in urban centres, they were visualised as places to which the non-churched many might be drawn in areas where they could most readily be encountered. When Hugh Price Hughes began the promotion of a number of such places up and down the land, the enterprise was seen as an aspect of ministering to the needs, spiritual and material, of people in cities, especially the poor and the underprivileged. Each was to be a focus of social and welfare work and each was also to be a place where the Gospel could be preached to those unlikely to enter a church of a more conventional kind.

The design and layout of such Central Halls were indicative of their function. Large—in some cases such as Birmingham and Nottingham—vast, they suggested auditoria rather than ecclesiastical buildings. They have been called 'open spaces with a roof'. They favoured tip-up seats rather than pews and behind or above was a complex of rooms and offices. The Central Halls of Methodism were thus large-scale enterprises, and to be minister of one required formidable energy and gifts. Whether their day is now over, due to sociological changes, as Donald long afterwards was to affirm and to get into trouble for so doing, does not invalidate the soundness of the original concept. But, in his view, the Central Hall in general had seen its greatest days by the time he left Islington in 1936. And now, many years later, though some continue to have much life, the echoing spaces of others do suggest that Donald's judgement in this matter, as in others of greater import, have proved correct even if unpopular.

But there was much to do at Islington in 1929. There were large congregations. At one stage there was a choir of ninety-five. There were Saturday evening concerts which for a time were a great success. There was a penny cinema every Saturday morning. There was a great community centre for some of the 7,000 unemployed in Islington. These were the bleakest days of the depression. Dole queues were everywhere, and all over the country men by the tens of thousands were suffering that slow erosion of self-respect, that bewildered bitterness which comes from being unwanted, which is the essence of unemployment. The young new minister of Islington Central Hall involved himself deeply in this situation. Men who came to the church to while away time found welcome and encouragement to fill it with craft and occupations provided. This, for Donald, was a rewarding exercise, as he put it. It certainly put him into contact with a great many people. For years it gave him a real insight into the harsh realities of social conditions as they were for many during those bleak times.

The film shows began as the result of an approach direct to Wardour Street which was the beginning of Donald's lifelong association with the world of mass-media. There occurred a few years later, on 10 June 1934 to be exact, another introduction to mass-media of greater import. At 8 p.m. on that Sunday he broadcast from St Martin-in-the-Fields at the invitation of H. R. L. Sheppard, still at that time its vicar. Thus began Donald's long association with the microphone. His ability to think on his feet, his splendid voice, before it was ruined by years of outdoor speaking, and his quick brain always primed with an awareness of what the headlines were saying at any particular moment, made him a natural for the medium. His abilities in this field have continued into the television age and, at any rate in terms of Christian comment on news and current affairs, he has had few equals.

But in 1934 radio, if just ceasing to be a novelty, was undoubtedly a power in the land and to be invited to speak on it, especially within the virtually sacred precincts of religious broadcasting, was an accolade. It could also be a daunting experience. Religion and politics were sensitive areas. Sometimes they became accidentally intermingled, so that Ramsay MacDonald himself on one occasion got into trouble over a travel talk called 'Forty Days and Forty Nights in the Sahara'. The title was considered blasphemous. Over all broadcasting, from his head office in Savoy Hill and later in Broadcasting House, down to the glowing-valved receiver in the humblest home, there brooded the personality of the BBC's first Director General, John Reith. He it was, this Prospero of the age, who saw to it that:

'. . . the isle is full of noises,
Sounds and sweet airs that give delight and hurt not.'

He was very keen to see that they hurt not. Dance bands were allowed, and the Savoy Orpheans, Paul Whiteman, Henry Hall and quite a few others came to fame by this means. But much good music was also brought into homes where before it had been unheard, and the admirable Sir Walford Davies taught many to appreciate it. Variety and concert parties, Sport and News, plays, even 'Recitations' were all allowed. Religious broadcasting was particularly allowed, and some, such as Harold Laski, thought there was too much of it. 'Sunday', he wrote in the *Daily Herald* in 1931, 'is what the lawyers call *dies non* on the wireless . . . we have endless sermons from St Martin-in-the-Fields. Could not Sir John risk a Communist?'

He at least risked Donald Soper, a Methodist speaking in an Anglican church, a daringly ecumenical act at that time.

Thus did Donald begin to encounter, as his activities broadened out during these years at Islington, some of the *dramatis personae* of the thirties. The high drama of the epoch, ending with a tremendous curtain in 1940, had a rich and varied cast. Some names are still evocative: the above-mentioned John Reith, ruling the air; Amy Johnson, the intrepid airwoman flying through it in her Gipsy Moth; Ramsay MacDonald, going on and on and up and up until he disappeared altogether; the red-headed Ellen Wilkinson leading the marchers from Jarrow; the poets Spender, Auden and MacNeice in tumultuous utterance over the Spanish Civil War; Baldwin, just as the demon kings, Hitler and Mussolini, were busy building them, saying that the bombers always got through; and then, finally, the disastrous Chamberlain on stage almost alone but for his umbrella, taking applause just before the curtain fell.

Meantime, these 'endless sermons from St Martin-in-the-Fields', to which Laski objected and Donald contributed, were a notable feature of the early thirties. In Dick Sheppard the BBC had found a broadcaster of genius. The fame of St Martin's, where he had built up a centre of Christian fellowship vividly alive and greatly admired, was a help. The very fact that Dick welcomed the microphone into his church was something of a breakthrough. The result had been a notable broadcasting ministry, and many people were helped by what came to them over the air from St Martin's at 8 p.m. on Sunday evenings. It is impossible to know, at this distance of time, what Donald said there on that June evening of 1934. But, since his basic attitudes and, indeed, mannerisms appear to have altered little over the years, it is likely that the close argument, the apt illustration, the unscripted fluency which have been features of his broadcasting ever since, were there then. But this was but one of the ways in which Donald's areas of operations widened during his nine years at Islington. At the same time his open-air ministry at Tower Hill was attracting growing attention. So, also, was his speaking at Highbury Corner, at one time an open-air forum as well known as Tower Hill itself. In Methodism he was already emerging as a figure of importance and his speaking was taking him up and down the country. At Islington Central Hall there was still much to be done. There was a very strong youth group there, and extensive social work, accentuated, as has been said, by the problems of care for the unemployed. In all these spheres it appeared that this young minister, handsome and forceful, was to be one of those people to whom success in most things came naturally.

Perhaps this was a highly important point in Donald Soper's life. The prospect lay before him of a continuing popularity among his own people within Methodism. They were grateful for him; they looked to him as a man of promise, as indeed he was. But, to fulfil that promise he would have had to conform to certain expected norms: to be eloquent, fervent, actively righteous. Indeed, all these conditions he satisfied. He was more than adequately equipped to be a luminary of this order as he grew older. But he was also much more, and it was these other elements in his character which, at this time, began to become noticeable to the public eye. He was a keen politician of the Left: he was an ardent pacifist: he got on splendidly with publicans and sinners, especially when arguing with them. On almost any issue of the day he could be guaranteed to have, not only an instant opinion, but usually a minority one, enunciated with a vigour and certitude which some found annoying.

For example, speaking at a public meeting in South London in 1937, he was reported as saying that he was a Socialist, a pacifist, that he had no use for a Christianity which said that the British Empire was the same as the Kingdom of God, and that he had no use for a Christianity which fought with thermite and mustard gas. As sentiments they were, as they still are, no doubt very sound, if, as to manner of expression, possibly a little immature. With the reference to Empire taken out, and thermite and mustard gas replaced by napalm and nuclear weapons, they could be made as relevant for today as yesterday. But in 1937 at any rate there was, surely, another side at least to the pacifist question, as the events of the next two years were to show.

But without any doubt, Donald made his mark during those seven years at Islington. Two years after he had gone from there to take up his life's work at the West London Mission centred on the Kingsway Hall, another paper summed up his achievement at Islington. 'It was during the early years of his work there that folk became aware of a new voice of power and influence in the religious life of the metropolis. In the midst of a population so nondescript as to include a good residential neighbourhood, another once middle-class but rapidly going downhill, and yet another typically working class, containing some very bad slums, Dr Soper thought that nothing but an institutional church in its widest sense could meet the need of the district. He was right.'

All these characteristics, and others, were to develop as time went by and grow more important as he became better known, so that Soper's dicta and views could be, and frequently were, taken by the general public to be those of the Methodist Church in general, rather than of one man in particular. This was especially so when he became President of Conference in the fifties. It would be easy to over-simplify this, and to represent Donald Soper as a progressive confronted by reaction. But it would not be the truth. Not a few of those annoyed by him from time to time were persons of integrity and high convictions themselves. But for the moment all this lay in the future. The point here is that he could have continued on from Islington as the golden boy of Methodism, or at any rate as one of them. Instead, he began to be, in terms of many of his opinions and attitudes towards the world at large which was always his primary concern, the odd man out.

. . . .

He was appointed Superintendent of the West London Mission in 1936. The importance of the move, and the high regard in which Donald was held at this time are both indicated by some of the press notices of the event. Thus: 'With the Revd D. Leslie Weatherhead at the City Temple and Dr Donald Soper at Kingsway, younger Methodist ministers will be holding two of the principal Free Church preaching stations in London. Dr Soper's reception at Kingsway had a wider significance than that of a Methodist welcome. At the inauguration, on Thursday, of the second year of the Youth and Citizenship movement, Dr Soper had a marked reception, indicating that he had completely captured Methodist sympathy. His speech was a masterpiece of logical and popular appeal, the latter relating to current problems, but the roots going deep into philosophy.'[1]

[1] *Christian World* (24.8.36).

There is even an air of hyperbole about some of the others. 'Londoners realise that the City possesses an open air preacher whose gifts have probably not been equalled since Hugh Latimer, in the reign of Henry VIII, addressed the crowds at Paul's Cross.'[1]

He had certainly entered upon a great inheritance—a phrase used by Dr Leslie Church in a short history of the West London Mission written to commemorate its jubilee in 1937. The phrase may seem unduly emotional. Most religious bodies, like political parties for that matter, tend to dramatise their actions and inflate their achievements. Even so, the beginnings of this West London Mission had grown out of a deep concern for the evil social conditions existing in the West End of the richest city in the world towards the close of the nineteenth century.

What some of these conditions were was revealed by a pamphlet written in the eighties by Andrew Mearns, Home Missions Secretary of the Congregational Church, *The Bitter Cry of Outcast London.* Poverty, prostitution, sickness, overcrowding, exploitation, loneliness and despair co-existed with the hansom cabs going to and fro among the money-making by day, and the glitter by night. W. T. Stead, editor of the *Pall Mall Gazette*, an outstanding journalist who was later to be the centre of a *cause célèbre* revealing some of the facts about the sale, and subsequent export to the Continent, of young girls for purposes of prostitution, gave Mearns's revelations wide publicity. Many were startled. Why they should have been so startled, and why these facts came as revelations, is yet another example of the isolation the British class system had encouraged. Most people—especially middle-class people—really did not realise how the other half lived, and the number of things about which respectability did not speak only increased the number of things about which respectability did not know.

'The middle classes as a rule have to combat innumerable prejudices, and are obliged to reject the traditions of their

[1] *British Weekly* (17.8.36).

infancy before they thoroughly comprehend the actual conditions of that race of people, which they are forced by immemorial prescription to regard as immensely inferior, if not altogether barbarous.'[1]

The moral and social condition of much of London had for a long time been chronic. Henry Mayhew himself, that prince of social investigators, had produced his four volumes of London Labour and the London Poor between 1851 and 1862. This lifted the curtain on the dark side of that town of which J. B. Priestley in *The Edwardians*, describing the kind of thing which Edward, Prince of Wales encountered in his youth writes, 'The London of the 1860s, much of it very disreputable indeed, might house Dickens's Mr Podsnap and his friends, worrying about anything that might "bring a blush into the cheek of a young person". But its customary late-night scenes were enough to embarrass the bosun of a whaling ship.'[2] William Booth's *In Darkest England* described it. Social workers in increasing numbers had exclaimed about it. But the majority of ordinary citizens either continued in ignorance or imagined that most of the misery was confined to the East End of the metropolis. This notion was prevalent when the Wesleyan Methodist minister, Hugh Price Hughes, read Mearns's pamphlet. He was deeply moved. Now when Hugh Price Hughes was deeply moved the results were likely to be epic. There was a great meeting in Exeter Hall with Lord Shaftesbury as chairman. The outcome was the beginning, against many odds, of the West London Mission. At its second anniversary, when Hughes said he wanted £50,000 for a suitable building, somebody laughed. Hughes turned on him at once. Had not the London Pavilion, a music hall, cost the same sum? The laugh was not repeated, and eventually Hughes got what he was seeking and, as a gift, St James's Hall in Piccadilly. The incident has a continuing significance as illustra-

[1] 'London Labour and London Poor,' quoted in *London's Underworld,* edited by Peter Quennell (Spring Books, 1966).
[2] J. B. Priestley, *The Edwardians* (Heinemann, 1970).

tive of something of the ethos of Missions such as this. They lived at war with what were clearly regarded as enemies, or at any rate as anti-social elements. Music halls were among them: so, pre-eminently, were pubs, often emotively referred to as gin palaces. So, by derivation, was most public entertainment. But the chief enemies were always poverty, squalor, sickness and the loneliness which came from rootlessness. It can be seen from this that Donald, with his stern temperance background, Puritan upbringing and marked social consciousness, was not moving to unfamiliar ground when he went to the West London Mission. There was an historic foundation already there upon which he could build his own modern structures. Political involvement was also no new thing, for the workers were encouraged from the start to interest themselves in civic affairs and local government. Ensor Walters, one of Donald's predecessors as Superintendent, was a member of the Borough Council of St Pancras and chairman of the Health Committee. Donald's membership in later times of the LCC, although it took many by surprise at the time, was in fact continuing a tradition rather than breaking new ground. Even his Socialism was to some degree within this tradition. Hughes himself had once said that the State, having passed Poor Laws, Factory Acts and Education Acts, must do its work thoroughly. If it was prepared to spend millions on defence against potential invaders, it ought to be prepared also to spend on defence against poverty which actually had invaded. These facts are important as answers to the charge, sometimes made, that Donald, with his many social and political commitments, was straying outside what some spoke of as the 'proper sphere' of the minister of the Gospel. But that, of course, is a very ancient stick with which to beat turbulent priests.

So the social work of this mission was of many kinds, and Donald found derivations or developments of most of them operating when he went there. Even Mrs Hugh Price Hughes herself, the formidable widow of the formidable founder, was still there in charge of the Sisterhood. But the premises had changed. When St James's Hall had been demolished in 1905 the mission had gone to Exeter Hall for a while, then to an old chapel in Great Queen Street. In 1909 the Lyceum Theatre was used for Sunday services. This was quite a sensation at the time, and the novelist Hall Caine wrote approving the enterprise and describing his impressions. And then, in 1912, the Kingsway Hall was opened. This was the place Donald went to in 1936, and it was to be the centre of his life and work henceforward, the base from which he exercised, as will be seen, a wide-ranging influence of many kinds. The building had seven floors, space for a gymnasium, clubs, schoolrooms, a lecture hall, an institute, Sisters' quarters, and the Crèche. The hall itself could hold 2,000 and, in the early days of Donald's ministry there, was accommodating 2,000 at Sunday services.

Donald set about the task before him with immense vigour. Before long, he had a band of young men visiting in Pentonville where he himself had been a nonconformist chaplain for some years. Inevitably, he had to make a joke even about that, remarking in a public speech about this time that there was a certain incongruity about hearing inmates of the prison singing the lines from the hymn 'Onward Christian Soldiers':

> Brothers we are treading
> Where the saints have trod.

Equally inevitably, and on a more serious note, he had to make a social comment, reporting the remark a diabetic prisoner had made to him that it was a strange sort of world in which, by producing a diabetic's card he could get insulin at any hospital, but could not get bread to eat at any baker's. 'One day', Donald said, in this long-forgotten address, 'we shall get compulsory free food', though what exactly was meant by the curious phrase seems unclear.

But what was very clear was the energy and purpose he brought to his work at Kingsway. The West London Mission was to be a great centre for social work: a place from which

Christian fellowship and conviction could reach out into the world. Soon, things began to happen. One who was there as a deaconess at the time recalled that 'Very soon D.O.S. (as we affectionately came to know him), inspired young men and women to accompany him to his open air work both at Hyde Park and Tower Hill. He had a great following from the very outset and out of this, and the enthusiasm of the young folk came the Order of Christian Witness.' That itself—the OCW—was a wide-ranging work destined to touch many lives before it faded with time and change. But the story of it, inasmuch as it goes far beyond the West London Mission, is part of the picture of Donald as a national figure, at any rate in Methodism, and must wait.

He was certainly beginning to be a national, even an international, figure outside Methodism as well. 1937, the year after he went to Kingsway, was a very full one. The tenth anniversary of his Tower Hill ministry was observed in April, when George Lansbury, full of years and Socialist honours, was one of the speakers. So was Hugh Redwood, author of a thirties best-seller, *God in the Slums*. In the same month, at a coronation celebration in Hyde Park, Donald shared the platform with Gipsy Smith and the Bishop of Kensington, which must have been an interesting conjunction. In July he sailed for South Africa and landed in trouble. Two thousand people gathered to hear him in Durban town hall on 'The Christian Answer to Communism and Fascism'. Some of his replies to questions were clearly not welcome to the audience. Pacifism and Socialism, it seems, were not attractive, to put it mildly, in South Africa even at that date, and the freedom of speech at Tower Hill in London did not easily export to Pretoria, Cape Town, Durban or Johannesburg.

Back home, he was soon planning a £10,000 scheme for the erection of a hostel for ex-prisoners from London, a hostel for girls, and a boys' club. All this was to mark the fiftieth anniversary of the Mission. The girls' hostel, to be named after Katherine Price Hughes, was started in Doughty Street, and became a home for girls on probation and in need of care and protection. It stayed in Doughty Street throughout the war, moving later to Highbury, in North London. Another need in these days was for a home in London where young students could live. Donald, who seemed to have a knack of finding the right person at the right time, contacted a man of property, Sir Malcolm Perks. The outcome was the acquisition of premises in Norland Square, Notting Hill. Two large houses were made into one, and an appeal from the pulpit in Kingsway furnished the place. The result was Fellowship House, which exists and flourishes to this day in Holland Park.

The backdrop to all this fervour and activity was, of course, the rapidly darkening international scene in these closing years of the thirties. For any man of Donald's pacifist convictions, they were bound to be times of particular stress. But the fact does not seem to have diminished either his fervour or the impact which he was beginning to make upon public life. What kind of a man, judging by his impact on others, was he at this time? What was the essence of the message which he clearly regarded himself as under a compulsion to proclaim, and what was he thinking of the way things were going? The three questions, if posed of Donald in the closing years of the thirties, and again, as they will be in this tale, at the beginning of the seventies, are likely to have much to say of at least one thinking Christian's progress through an extraordinary period in which two of the many ideological casualties have been the decline of certitudes in general, and the accompanying and related decline of institutional Christianity.

What kind of a man, then, was he at this time, judging by his effect on others? (His effect, it seems, could not only be considerable; but take at times odd forms. A stained-glass window, one of the lights in which depicted him speaking on Tower Hill, was unveiled in a Muswell Hill Methodist church in 1937.) A less unusual picture of him, however, is to be found in a description of him by a writer in a north-country newspaper, in

June 1938. 'In my young days the preachers were almost entirely great theologians or great pulpit figures. I would not put Dr Soper down as either. True enough, he is a fine speaker, indeed a natural orator, with a most attractive voice, as those who have so often heard him on the wireless well know. He can, and does, preach a powerful and challenging, invigorating sermon. But his principal characteristics are in my own view none of these. Beyond everything else he is a great social evangelist, an inspirer and leader of men in action, one of the most significant figures in the religious life not only of Great Britain but of the English-speaking world.'

The article itself goes some way to answering the second question, as to the nature of Donald's message at this time. 'The revolutionary nature of Christianity and the profound significance of conversion were two important features in Dr Donald Soper's message.

'He had very little patience and even less understanding of those people who talked of religion as though it were a personal thing with social implications. It was both—personal and social—and to over-emphasise one to the neglect of the other was a comment upon the failure of churches down the centuries. . . . Christianity was above all a revolutionary doctrine.'

Extracts, of course, are inevitably misleading. Some are even unfair. Thus; 'Speaking of the presence of God in mankind, he remarked that if he could not believe that there was something of God in Hitler and Mussolini, then of all men he would be most miserable.'

But the overall impression is one of certitude. Christianity was not only a revolutionary doctrine: it was the answer to the needs of a stricken world. 'What we could not do, Christ could do for us.' A long time afterwards, in another age, almost another world, this same Donald Soper was, as will be shown, very sharply critical of the American Billy Graham for saying some not dissimilar things, a fact surely not indicative so much of inconsistency as of development.

The third question remains: what was Donald thinking within himself as the scene darkened? For him, about this time, it darkened not only internationally; but in two personal respects as well. His younger brother 'Sos', Meredith Ross, by that time a master at Kings College, Wimbledon, died suddenly at the age of twenty-six. The profound effect of this upon Donald has already been mentioned. In addition, he fell ill himself, quite seriously so. It began with appendicitis, and he had the routine operation at St Mary's Hospital, Paddington. But complications set in, and he was immobilised with a potentially dangerous thrombosis for six months. This was a severe trial. Inactivity, then as always, was one of the few things which for Donald was unbearable. This was not necessarily a virtue; some people found it an annoyance that he seemed incapable of being still for a while. But now he had to be, and the experience gave rise to an interesting self-revelation in a radio programme thirty-one years later.

Asked what, of all his life's experiences, was that which had given him most delight, he replied: 'I was on my back once for six months, and I was thoroughly miserable. But it had one tremendous effect upon me. I found out during those six months what I really most wanted to do, what was really at the centre of my life. It was to climb the steps of Kingsway Hall and to stand in the pulpit and conduct public worship. The happiest moment of my life was when I tottered up those steps. I don't pretend I'm pious; but that was heaven for me. That was where I knew I ought to be, however badly I did it.'[1]

When eventually he returned to Kingsway Hall the occasion was one of some warmth. 'Dr Soper was on the Kingsway Hall platform again on Sunday night and a subdued murmur greeted his appearance. It was known that he wanted no sentiment. Sympathetic eyes, however, watched his painful climb up the steps, notwithstanding his effort to hide every sign of infirmity. He had left his two sticks in the minister's vestry. Dr Soper was obviously reluctant to speak of his personal experiences. But

[1] BBC programme 'Five to Ten' (5.1.69).

lying under all he said were the reflections of quiet hours in the hospital and at home. He had been going over his life, his theology and his preaching message. So much was plain, and on his first reappearance on the Kingsway platform he could utter only his deepest thoughts. He confessed himself frankly appalled at the state of the world. He had come out of his silence with the impression that this time British statesmen would not successfully muddle through. As the months had passed, he had not found it easy to lie in bed and hope. His second unchangeable belief was that redemption began with the individual. Here was to be found the initial field for evangelism. The greatest contribution one could make to the advancement of the Kingdom of God was his own changed life.'[1]

It was, and it remained, his basic theme—this kingdom of God. It was real: it was attainable. Righteousness and social justice were some of the powers leading towards it: and few things have done more to emasculate the Christian religion than the removal of the Kingdom into a never-never land of nebulosity. In a small book, actually a collection of radio addresses, *Popular Fallacies*, first published in 1938, he developed this theme in a passage which contains a considerable part of his credo. 'The fallacy which meets the Christian advocate at every point is the idea that this Kingdom of Heaven is really only a kind of metaphor like the "Garden of Happiness" or the "Land of Hearts Desire". If it helps to think of such a realm, of the bright blue sky, no harm is done; it is just a pious fantasy which may comfort the believer. But it has no meaning except as a kind of spiritual asylum for the weary spirits of those who find life hard and disappointing. Its practical value is precisely limited to the personal happiness it gives to those who find satisfaction in a world of make-believe, and name their little home in a London back street "Clovelly", or "Windyridge". . . but the Kingdom of God is both a personal and a social realm. The kingdom is set up in you and me when our hearts are warmed by the love

[1] *Methodist Recorder* (22.12.38).

of God, our wills are loyal to his will, and our desire is to serve him. This is the Kingdom of Heaven which in the words of Jesus is within you—the reign of God in each of us.'[1]

But any kind of Kingdom of Heaven, personal or social, seemed far away indeed as the autumn of 1939 approached. When the sirens eventually sounded on 3 September, just after eleven in the morning, it seemed for a moment as if everybody, after the garrulous thirties, had suddenly to stop talking and apply themselves to other matters. The People's War, as Angus Calder was long afterwards, in a notable book, to call it, had begun. Within eighteen months Donald, along with some other notables, was blacklisted by the BBC. Some of the press was quite excited about this. 'The BBC is extending its anti-pacifist blockade. It has now blacklisted three famous preachers—Dr Donald Soper, of Kingsway Hall and Tower Hill; Dr George MacLeod, of Iona; and Canon Charles Raven, Regius Professor of Divinity at Cambridge. Dr Soper, of the Methodist West London Mission, is one of the most popular religious broadcasters in Britain, and his numerous microphone talks, especially his question and answer series on Sunday afternoons, reached an immense public.'

It was to be some years before he was to be heard over the air again. Instead, as time wore on, he was attended by a Special Branch man, presumably interested in possible sedition, sometimes on Tower Hill. This man took down his speeches. When occasionally, after a burst of rapid speech, Donald felt that there might have been difficulty for this individual in getting it all down, he would pause to let him catch up. But that lay in the future. For the moment, there was more than enough to do at Kingsway Hall.

[1] *Popular Fallacies About the Christian Faith* (Hodder & Stoughton, 1938).

# 4

# The Man in the Headlines

> London's most promising newcomer in the battle for the headlines is a challenger in the People's Oracle class. Dr Donald Soper, fifty-year-old President of the Methodist Conference, earns bigger and blacker type by speaking his mind.
>
> *Evening Standard* (4.12.53)

> Those who are pioneers are not only expected to blaze a trail, and undertake rigours of discipline which other people do not have to undertake; but they are also those who must keep steadily before them the object of their journey, and see by faith the end of the road.
>
> D.O.S. in Address to Conference at end of his Presidential Year, 1954

THE WAR did not change Donald's pacifism. Angus Calder names him as one of three public figures who were equally unbending. Many had felt revulsion against war: it had been a marked feature of the thirties. But now, 'some of those who had led that revulsion—notably Bertrand Russell and C. E. M. Joad—had now decided that Nazism must be resisted by force. Other distinguished men and women—the Bishop of Birmingham, Dame Sybil Thorndike, the Methodist leader Donald Soper—maintained their pacifism throughout the war. Yet their choice was uncomfortable to sustain, as news came from Europe of the fate of the Jewish communities.'[1]

This total pacifism of Donald's is such a large matter, covers such a sweep of years, and raises so many issues, that it will need to be examined separately, as a major part of the picture of the man. It needs to be born in mind, however, as the constant background to the tale of the West London Mission in that

[1] Angus Calder, *The People's War* (Jonathan Cape, 1969).

testing time. One of the three Wesley Deaconesses of the day, Sister Hudd, later Mrs C. M. Lloyd, recalled some of it in a memoir evocative of the now almost forgotten atmosphere of that People's War.

'When the bombing began, or even before, changes had to be made at Kingsway. The first of these was to get the Crèche out of London. Apart from Emerson Bainbridge Hostel, the other hostels were able to stay open. Almost at once two centres for feeding got under way. One was on the first floor in the suite of rooms known as the Community Centre, and here the girls from Bainbridge House ate, and were soon joined by the Firewatchers in the neighbouring offices. They were most glad to be able to come in for breakfast and rest before beginning their day's work. This service grew into providing hot lunches and evening meals to office workers from around the hall.

'Every day, at some time during the meal Dr Soper would walk through the room, stopping to chat, or sometimes he would sit at the piano and play. This friendliness was greatly appreciated, and he gained some real supporters of the Mission in this way. The other feeding centre was set up in the lecture hall on the ground floor to serve breakfasts to a great number of people who had sheltered overnight in the Holborn Underground station, or in the Masonic Hall in Great Queen Street. Every morning at 6.30 the doors were opened; the people streamed in and were able to have a hot breakfast before going to work or to their homes. Young helpers of these projects slept in the bunks in Kingsway Hall. They were mostly conscientious objectors and several made a permanent home with us, going home at the weekends if they were able. Dr Soper was a great friend and fortifier to these young men, attending with them at their Tribunals, although not always helping them by so doing. As you will know, he had his enemies, and they could well be serving on one or other of these Tribunals. Not all of his staff, either, shared his views; but that did not prevent them from giving him full support during these trying years. One could only admire the work which he inaugurated and so well supported himself in easing the lot of the local civilians caught up in the war.

'One outstanding episode of these days was when, after an extensive raid on the Theobalds Road area, over four hundred people flocked to the Hall. Our water and gas were off; but as soon as it was safe a tap was set up in the road operated by Dr Soper and the human chain and runners kept this going until services could be restored. A wonderful spirit of camaraderie existed. Another time a bomb dropped on a block of flats in Peabody Building, just behind the Hall, and Dr Soper went out with all the men on the premises to help to pull the people from the wreakage. It proved a gruesome business and a sad time for those who had lost their homes and who came drifting in to us.'

One special piece of work which Donald undertook in conjunction with the then vicar of St Martin in the Fields, Eric Loveday, was a shelter for vagrants from the Embankment. A place was found for them under Hungerford Arches, Charing Cross. The eventual outcome of this, after the war, was that the LCC offered an old Poor Law institution in Lambeth as a permanent home for those men and women. This became the Hungerford Club. Some of the young people who had looked after these folks through the war gladly became the first members of its staff. The Hungerford operated until 1948 as a come-and-go home for these vagrants. When the need for it on these lines faded with time it was replaced by a home for discharged prisoners until they could sort themselves out. A house was found in Camden Town and adapted for this work, and continued to operate until other interested bodies joined forces and established a permanent home in Highbury. The character of the Hungerford changed again when, after structural alterations to make it more habitable, it became a home for alcoholics; men at first, then another house for women: St Luke's and St Mary's. But this was a development which came long after the war.

Such is a modest account of what was in fact a fairly heroic time at Kingsway, as at other places. Another question altogether is what was Donald saying as a Christian leader, and as a pacifist, in these times. The various answers give some indication of the principles he worked to. Preaching on the second Sunday of the war, he said that, 'absolute pacifists, like himself, should in peace strive against war, and in war devote themselves to the service of the people. Christian people were caught in a social machine. They could not carry out their desires because of what others did. They had freedom for one thing, however, and that was doing good. Good deeds for men opened doors through which God came into the world.' And what was happening at Kingsway in May 1940, when the world seemed to be falling apart with the German invasion of the Low Countries and France? One observer went along to see. 'At Kingsway Hall there was not a vacant seat. Dr Donald Soper said that from reports he had received from every part of London, north and south of the Thames, places of worship had been crowded that day. If those who now thronged the churches had thronged them during the last twenty years they would not now be meeting in such circumstances as had at last brought them together. The spiritual potency and power which could be generated and utilised in such services as that one were equal to the task of establishing and maintaining on earth peace and truth and all those lovely things which now seemed so remote.'

By the November of the same year a grimmer picture was to be seen, 'It is Sunday night in the heart of London. The guns are booming overhead and there is the constant hum of planes. Down on the lower floor of a great Methodist building a crowd of business men and women are gathered round the fire. Dr Soper is at the piano. Hymn after hymn is being sung, until it seems as though the group must know the whole hymn book by heart. On Monday morning these young people will be up long before daylight serving breakfast to hundreds of people who have slept in the tubes and shelters. Work such as this is of the very essence of the spirit which has lived in the West London Mission throughout its fifty years of service.'

And so the work continued through the changes and chances of those years. There can be no doubt that Donald, very much an odd man out as regards his personal attitude, was an inspirer and leader in the front line of his own position and work. He was also, inevitably, much disliked and suspected by some. He said, 'I preached pacifism on Tower Hill for the whole of the war. I once received a message, strangely enough, from Sangster, who said that he had been instructed to tell me that they would be loath to put me in prison. I told him that he should have said more or less than that; but as it was I was not interested and I heard no more of it.'

That passionate kind of hostility mellowed with time, and other concerns took its place. One idea—baffling because so much out of character in a man who had always had so little time for buildings, and so strong a desire to take his message out of them—which Donald himself seems to have held at this time was a plan for a Methodist Cathedral on a site near the Marble Arch. It seemed incredible; but there it is, in the London *Evening News* of 23 September 1944. 'The scheme might cost £200,000, or even half a million, Dr Soper said today. "We want to build something more than just another church", he said. "A cathedral type of church is a possibility, with the doors wide open to everyone and sufficient freedom to be a contribution to church unity." '

However, it did not happen and may be relegated to the faded file wherein are still to be found outlines of schemes which many were thinking up when the approaching end of war gave rise to the customary dreams, invariably vain, of a new world after it.

But one scheme did seem to be working out. 'Dr Soper's dream', said Sister Hudd, 'of making the West London Mission a great centre for social work was coming true. There were, however, still one or two gaps. He wanted a holiday home. At the same time a group of elderly persons who were finding the housing shortage difficult approached him. Dr Soper put their needs to a property man with whom he had become friendly, stressing that the holiday home was to come first. Soon this friend came up with an offer of a house on Sydenham Hill, which the owner was willing to give to the Mission. This became the home for the elderly and retired, and many of them are living there happily to this day. The holiday home was found on the front at Worthing, and was fitted up to give pleasure to as many as wished. It was in great demand for a number of years; but as the need became less apparent, it was sold.'

So it was, and is a detail of some significance. Never the man to hold on to anything once he felt it had served its purpose, Donald had no compunction in getting rid of it. In a sense, indeed, much of his life seems to have been an exercise in the unloading of inessentials once he had become convinced that they were so. To apply the principle to buildings is one thing; to apply it to matters of doctrine and belief is another, and not the least of the importance and relevance of his story is to discover how much, as the years passed, of doctrine and belief he felt it necessary to dispense with on the same grounds of redundancy.

The same Deaconess who remembered Kingsway in wartime, and who became Sister-in-Charge in 1947 when the last of the old order of West London Sisters died, was in a position to see Donald at close quarters in these years. Outwardly, he appeared at the height of his powers, filled with confidence, energy and ideas. He had one of the largest congregations in London on Sunday evenings. Kingsway had a band of young people who, with prison and hospital visiting, staffing in some cases the various hostels of the Mission, serving in the community centre, going with him to Tower Hill and Hyde Park, were excitingly challenged all the time. Sometimes they were asked to do unusual things. One was to befriend the island of Antigua, many years before it was to break into the news in the late sixties. Donald, visiting the place on one of his post-war preaching and lecturing tours, noticed its poverty and came back to form 'The Friends of Antigua' from among the young people at Kingsway. A house on the island at that time cost £150. Soon this was raised, and so were some houses.

Such was but one among the many enterprises which sprang from this incredibly active Superintendent of the West London Mission. He was very much a public figure; he was becoming a world traveller, as will appear. He seemed increasingly to be one who startled people by his views. But there were considerable differences, it seemed, between this rather brash and ebullient controversialist and the kind of person he really was behind the façade. 'I knew him to be', his sometime Sister-in-Charge wrote, 'a very sensitive man. Probably that is contrary to what most people thought. He could be deeply moved. I think, too, that he was a humble man. I know him to have been a very patient man, able to wait quietly for an opportunity and then, when it came, to grasp it with determination. I never knew him to lose his temper, although I guess he was often very tried. I have seen him deeply annoyed, especially if a young man tried to imitate him. That was the one thing he could not tolerate. He had all the patience in the world for those in real trouble, and when he was not able to help he put them in touch with someone who could. He did not spare himself when interviewing people, and I have known him to carry on to the point of exhaustion. He is a man of his word, and once a promise is given then it is fulfilled, no matter how difficult. My husband said that his most vivid picture of a beloved Superintendent is of him kneeling at the Communion Table.'

In 1952, by a majority of eighteen votes of the second ballot at the Methodist Conference of that year at Preston, Donald was designated for the presidency of Conference in 1953. It was the highest honour his church could bestow upon him.

. . . .

The height, however, should not be exaggerated. A man is President for a year. At the end of his term of office he returns, without ceremony, whence he came and to what he was, in accordance with the honourably plain traditions of the Methodist ministry. Even the procedure of election reflects the intention to be truly democratic. So the voting for President Designate is by members of the Representative Session, ministers and laymen and women, without any public nomination. There are slips of paper in the agenda, and each member is invited to name the man he wants. About a dozen names mostly appear, and are announced to the Conference. Then the voting takes place between the two or three highest numbers. This, then, is what happened to Donald at Preston. The first act of the 1953 Conference at Birmingham was accordingly to elect him President. This having been done, a droll exchange took place between the outgoing President and Donald, an exchange interesting as yet another example of his apparently incurable addiction to mingling levity with solemnity. 'It's is my great pleasure and privilege', said the outgoing President, at the end of a moving allocution, 'to induct you to this office, and to commit you to the prayers of the Methodist people. I have to hand to you, sir, this symbol of our office, John Wesley's Bible. I know that your whole life will be sustained by the truth it contains.' To this Donald replied; 'In trying, sir, to thank you very inadequately on behalf of us all, I found some words in the Conference Agenda which I propose to read. They are, "At 3.15, 214 for 3". I beg your pardon, those are the numbers of two hymns.' (They were in fact the current Test score.) He continued, 'I shall not detain the Conference at this stage with many words. But you will recognise, I think, the sincerity of my feelings when I say that this office comes to me with a great sense of surprise—a sense of surprise shared by many others. Somewhat presumptuously, sir, a little while ago, I was reminded of the frailty of human wishes when I bought my Presidential suit. Within a week the house was burgled and the suit was taken. I have looked carefully around Conference and, as far as I can see, it is not here, although I have not yet scrutinised the platform.' And then, abruptly changing gear, he concluded, 'I shall try, sir, to do my best. I shall try to do my best because I believe in Jesus Christ. And I cannot let this moment pass without remembering the gladness which comes to my aged parents—my mother, who is here, and my father who is too crippled to come.'

So there he was, with the customary large Presidential itinerary of visits to churches before him, the customary heavy involvement in the major committees of the Church, and the responsibility, among much else, of being regarded, at any rate by the outer world, as the chief spokesman of that Church. How he met that responsibility, and how he reached the headlines with views and dicta on an extraordinary variety of topics, thus earning the title, from one paper, of a 'People's Oracle', will shortly be told.

But, before that, a deeper matter needs, in justice, to be looked at. It is the question as to what kind of a Christian in general, and what kind of a Methodist in particular, he was at this time and henceforward. Anyone who has lived as Donald had, involved daily with the world's passing show, is always in danger of being thought of as a man lacking roots in the things which do not pass away. Eric Baker, that same Secretary of Conference who has been quoted before, put it this way: 'Just as so many people think of him as the espouser of causes rather than as one who renders personal service, so it is very easy for his own intense religious life and spirituality to escape the notice of people. However, anyone who has ever been present when he has given a charge to Ordinands at a Methodist Ordination service will have seen an aspect of Donald which does not often find public expression, but which is perhaps as complete a revelation of the true man, of the very core of his being, as one could ever have. Those who have heard this would all say that Donald's Ordination charges are among the most wonderful religious utterances that it has been their privilege to hear, and that they spring from a deep devotion and spirituality that tend to escape notice because of other, more exciting facets of his personality, which are more superficial yet which first of all attract attention.

'He is a believer in the great historic creeds, and yet not in any wooden way. He has on more than one occasion professed that he cannot hold the doctrine of the Virgin birth. Yet he is a Methodist high churchman in a very real sense, President of the Methodist Sacramental Fellowship, one who places the Communion Service at the very heart of Christian worship. When he was President of Conference and went round the circuits of Methodism, as presidents do, he insisted that everywhere he went they should hold a Communion Service, and very often after that service he led the people out to an act of open-air witness and proclamation. More than that, it must never be thought that this espousal of causes means that causes mean more to him than people. Donald is not a professional psychologist or psychotherapist. But I am sure that more people have turned to him for help and found more, in this field, than many a professional psychologist could claim. He knows what is in man; he understands people and is able to put his finger on the root trouble of people's disabilities and mental illnesses in a most remarkable way.'

The Sacramental Fellowship mentioned is important to the overall picture of Donald as a Methodist. Stewart Denyer, its chairman, had revealing things to say on the matter. 'It was founded in 1935, and Donald became its third President in 1950. He had not then, I think, been a member for long, and after the lull in its activity during the war, his acceptance of the appointment was really an affirmation of the Fellowship's vital interest in the mission of the Church to the post-war world. Writing in the bulletin of the MSF, Donald said that effective evangelism must be based upon a clear recognition of what Christianity is, "It must spring from, and lead to, the Christian Church. The sacrament of the Lord's Supper provides the authentic and actual means whereby decision can be expressed and discipleship begun in the Christian life". Like his predecessor at Kingsway

Hall, Hugh Price Hughes, and like the Wesleys, Donald said he had found in the Eucharist a converting ordinance, the mainspring of the Church's mission to individual sinners and to mankind. In 1953, when he was President of the Methodist Conference, he called on Methodists to make the same rediscovery. Throughout his year of office he insisted on making the celebration of Holy Communion the main feature of his visits to churches and circuits, instead of the "preaching service" which had hitherto been customary for the President's visit. I think this deep sacramentalism and high doctrine of the Church have often been forgotten or unknown by those who think of Donald Soper mainly as a Socialist and a pacifist. Those of us who share his other enthusiasms are glad that they are really based upon this theological foundation. He is, of course, very much of a liberal Catholic, as we used to call them, and as his age would suggest. Some members of MSF have been a little shaken occasionally with his apparently light treatment of the Bible. But these are, I think, rather remnants of the 1920s' liberalism, and he is content to join heartily in the creeds as battle-cries of the faith and of the Church, rather than as intellectual exercises.'

The suspicion which this sacramental emphasis at times aroused deserves a word of explanation. 'I think perhaps the objection to the Methodist Sacramental Fellowship', wrote Dr Harold Roberts, 'was that there were those who felt that there was a real danger of isolating the sacraments from the life of the Church as a whole. There is always a danger lest the Church should be identified with part of its doctrine and not with the whole. And it will be found that the resistance was due to the fear that Methodism was becoming a sacramental church in the sense of a sacerdotal church. You still find people using the word sacerdotal to mean that the Church was becoming priest-ridden. And so the Sacramental Fellowship, it was thought, was opening the door to conceptions of the ministry and, indeed, to priestly assumptions, which would not, at any rate, be very acceptable to a large number of Methodists.'

That it was not always acceptable was a fact reflected in correspondence from time to time. Thus in May 1951, Donald as President and Dr D. Sharp as Secretary of the MSF felt moved to reply to critical letters which had been appearing in the *Methodist Recorder*. 'Regarding our alleged over-emphasis of the Sacrament, we merely insist that the Holy Communion should have its proper place as the focal point of our worship . . . we make no apology for these views, for we are proclaiming real Methodism as proclaimed by John and Charles Wesley. We would only quote, "Jesus, we thus obey thy last and kindest word; here, in thine own appointed way, we come to meet thee, Lord".'

Much odder and very different grounds for suspicion of Donald arose from his sartorial habits, which included the habitual wearing of a cassock or, alternatively and often, a light suit and a red tie. Many years later, incidentally, the cassock was a source of particular aggravation to some of the disciples of the Reverend Ian Paisley, when Donald visited Belfast in the late sixties.

But undoubtedly the Sacramental Fellowship, with its three aims: to reaffirm the faith of the catholic creed which inspired the Methodist revival; to restore to Methodism the sacramental worship of the universal Church as set forth in the lifelong practice and teachings of the Wesleys; and the corporate reunion of all believers, was, and remained, very important to Donald as an unchanging emphasis within his ministry.

So also was the Order of Christian Witness, formed in 1946. This was a very considerable work. Inspired by Donald, and for years led by him, it touched the lives of many people deeply. Its purpose was to enable lay people, led by their minister, working in teams, living in community and paying their own way, to go out on an annual campaign, with the object of witnessing, wherever they were invited, to the faith that was in them. Obviously, this is of importance to the picture of Donald as a Methodist and to his attitude to evangelism. This could be summed up in a sentence of his; 'We must begin with people where they are, and not where we would like them to be.' Long afterwards, his aversion to mass evangelism led to a clash with the American Billy Graham, and the reason for the clash lay in these words.

But the significance of this Order of Christian Witness goes beyond such limited considerations. In its rise upon a tide of idealism, its persistence in face of odds, and then its gradual decline, it seems to speak of the high mortality rate of most spiritual endeavours in this latter part of the twentieth century. A social worker, Sister Lewis, discovered in South London recently, made, if unconsciously, this point very clear.

'The Order of Christian Witness really first began at Kingsway Hall among a group of the young people just at the beginning of the war. I think it largely grew out of the frustration of a group of pacifists feeling that there was nothing that they could do. Finally they decided that they would go down to Dorking, speaking in the open air, sleeping on church premises, and generally carrying out an evangelistic campaign. In subsequent years, this same group from Kingsway carried on this work. In 1945 every Methodist minister in the London area received a letter from Dr Soper asking if anyone was interested in this kind of thing, and if so would they meet at the Kingsway Hall. From that meeting it was arranged that we should have a week's campaign in Salisbury in 1945. We were then known as the London Christian Campaigners and that week, I think for all of us who went, was one of the memorable weeks of our lives. It was the first big campaign, and because we interested people, it was decided at the end, when we came back to make future plans, that the name had to be changed, and it was in 1946 that the first Order of Christian Witness campaign was held. I myself went for twenty-one years without a break and then felt that I had probably done it for long enough, although I confess I miss it still from time to time.

'On a campaign, we were normally divided into groups called Family Groups, billeted in local churches. The group gathered together on a Saturday. On the Sunday we all went out and took services in many churches and then the rest of the week preached Christ to anyone who would listen. We did open-air work of course, because this was one of Dr Soper's great things, and every one of us who went on campaign, even if we weren't prepared for this, normally ended up by doing it. We also went out looking for groups of people, spoke in factories and canteens, and house groups, later on, did a lot of work. From the very beginning, Dr Soper was the leader of the campaigns and we were all really obedient to what he told us to do. There was a wonderful sense of community and of following and of believing implicitly in what the leader said. I think everyone who went on campaigns loved him. The most wonderful part of any campaign was always evening prayers, when we all gathered together. These have left wonderful memories. I have never known anything quite like them. Particularly in the early years of campaigns—it was just at the end of the war—there was a terrific spirit of hope. The war had finished: here was a new world: the campaigners were young: some of them had been through part of the war, many of them had grown up during the war and now they were ready to serve their country in a new and better way. This went on through the 1950's but gradually it changed, and it is difficult to know why. I think that we have lost something, and that perhaps the time is coming when we should realise this and begin to think again.'

There was one matter, however, which Donald himself never seems to have felt any need to rethink. This was his uncompromising Puritanism. No picture of him as a man, as a Methodist, as a public figure or indeed as anything else would approach accuracy unless this were made clear. The difficulty is that this rigorous attitude of mind has generally been concealed by a sophisticated outward appearance and charm of manner. People meeting the Donald Soper of the light suit and the red tie, the informed conversation, can be surprised to discover, should some apposite issue arise, that they are also face to face

As it was in the beginning. Tower Hill in the twenties
(Photo: Keith Ellis)

Soper in stained glass: a window, unveiled in 1937, in Muswell Hill Methodist Church. The top light depicts Donald on Tower Hill (Photo: E.W. Tattersal)

The argument continues. Discussing Pacifism with John Middleton Murry for an article in *Picture Post*, 5 August 1950 (Photo: Hulton Press Ltd., *Picture Post*)

President of Conference, 1953
(Photo: E.W. Tattersal)

With students of Ibadan University

Speaking in Manchester, 1955: a typical attitude
(Photo: Topical Press Agency Ltd.)

Forty years on: Speakers' Corner, Hyde Park (Photo: John Ray Photography, *Methodist Recorder*)

The protestor: 'H Bomb' vigil at US Embassy (Photo: PA-Reuter Photos Ltd)

Lunch-hour dialogue at St Mary-le-Bow, Cheapside
(Photo: Keith Ellis, *Methodist Recorder*)

Lady Marie Soper admires her husband's World Peace Award, October 1981, in London, following the presentation by Bishop William Cannon of the American United Methodist Church (Photo: Keith Ellis)

with a man whose views on such things as drink and gambling have about as much give as reinforced concrete. That taciturn sometime-President of the United States, Calvin Coolidge, upon being asked on one occasion what had been the theme of the sermon he had that morning heard, replied 'Sin'. Being asked to elucidate somewhat the attitude of the preacher who had developed this theme, he is said to have replied, 'He was against it'.

Similarly, as regards quite a number of what have now become widely accepted social habits, especially drinking and gambling, it could be said that Donald Soper is against them. The list could be extended to include blood sports and smoking, among other things. The more society grows permissive, the more isolated such a position inevitably becomes, and the value of its witness, possibly, increases. Be that as it may, this is something unchanging in Donald, not as a manifestation of narrow-mindedness so much as an expression of self-dedication maintained with formidable resolution. In an address to the Methodist Conference at the conclusion of his year of office as President, on the theme of Christian morality, he made his position clear.

'I want to set this argument for morality and for discipline in the right perspective. You cannot be a Christian without being a moral disciplinarian, for yourself and for others. My reason for being a teetotaller is that drink keeps millions of my fellow creatures out of the Kingdom of God. My reason for having nothing to do with gambling is that it is an anti-social device whereby some people get richer and most people get poorer. It is, in other words, the distribution of wealth according to an anti-social principle, and anyone who is concerned about a better world should have nothing to do with it. It is one of the supreme facts that in human life it is personal discipline which is the recall to God and which makes every day a sacred day. It is that constant recall to God which is so necessary and so little realised. . . . Our moral discipline is the golden chain that binds us about the feet of God and brings us ever, even in our temptations and difficulties, to the throne of grace, where we have health and comfort and, ultimately, victory.'

The Donald Soper who could speak thus seems a long way from the controversial Soper of the headlines. Yet it was there, none the less, that, for better or for worse, he chiefly came upon the public scene, offering instant comment, usually of a provocative nature, upon the events and issues of the day. Some have found this irritating. Others have found it so interesting as to inquire into the motives of a man who seemed to have so much to say about so many things. One of these interested parties was a writer in the London *Evening Standard* during Donald's Presidential year. Under the heading 'Soper's Soapbox' was this:

'In the past few months Soper has hit the front page by criticising the Queen, for going to the races; Prince Philip, for playing polo on Sundays; the Army, in Kenya; gambling, anywhere. He has been saying similar things for about twenty-five years. Now in newspaper libraries he has graduated to the large-size cutting envelopes, still columns behind the Archbishop of Canterbury, who rates eleven envelopes, but soon due to a box for himself. Is he a headline seeker because he likes publicity? Not likely. Straight publicity-mongers sing their songs in harmony with public opinion. Is he just a meddlesome crank who wants to pry into everyone's life and make people live his own way rather than their own? Some people will say so. But he is more than that. He does want people to think his way. "Of course I do." he says, "but I want to persuade them to think my way. To do that I must first of all make them think. That is what I want to do." '

It is doubtful, however, if the answer goes far enough. Beyond the desire to make people think has surely always been, for Donald, the even more ardent desire to make it quite plain there is no area of human life to which the Christian faith is irrelevant. Advocates of the notion that religion should keep clear of world affairs have rarely had a stouter opponent. So everything was open to Christian comment, and no holds were barred. The results, given by a random sample of press cuttings of the fifties, are startling. Here was a Don Quixote who charged every windmill in sight. The odd thing is that some, by this time, had been revealed not as windmills at all; but as real causes of concern now generally accepted as such. He was, for instance, in 1957 condemning smoking in terms now used by the BMA. 'For long enough now a statistical relationship between heavy smoking and lung cancer has been established beyond doubt. The probability that many smokers have already contracted the preliminary stages of cancer is only sightly less calamitous than the certainty that many young people are now busy producing bodily conditions which will eventually kill them in twenty years time.'

In 1955, in the same paper, *Tribune*, he was criticising Church and State relationships along lines very similar to those followed in the official Anglican report of 1970. 'Let the Church of England demand that the Sovereign take the advice of men selected by the Church itself. There are no grounds for a divorce between Church and State. But there is a case for restitution of conjugal rights.'

In 1957 he was welcoming the Wolfenden Committee's Report on Homosexual Offences and Prostitution by advocating the more tolerant and understanding attitude to the homosexual condition now taken for granted. 'I believe the Report will give a sense of hope and a promise of justice to a great many homosexuals in this country who are honestly trying to live straight and decent lives, in conditions which have been almost intolerable.'

This prescience did not prevent him, however, from bringing in pacifism, even into this context. 'My personal view is that the root of perversion is violence. I believe that a disarmed world would be a world in which homosexuality would die out. I believe that if we could get rid of power politics and conscription we should get rid of sexual perversion.'

This remarkable opinion could be equalled by similar statements involving, in equally unexpected contexts, capitalism. Thus, condemning professional boxing, he said: 'Boxing is very unworthy to be called sport. It is a serious menace to the health of those who take part in it. It is a capitalistic racket for those who promote it, and it stimulates perversion, sexual and otherwise, in those who watch it.' Like Mr Dick in *David Copperfield*, with his obsession with King Charles's head, Donald does seem to have had something not dissimilar in his attitude to these issues. But of the prophetic nature of some of his statements there can be little doubt, then or later. When, in 1971, the selection of a wrong tape by an American defence installation in the heart of Cheyenne Mountain, responsible for warning of nuclear attack, caused an alert to be inadvertently broadcast nationwide, except by the numerous radio stations which fortunately ignored it, Donald, in a passionate article in *Tribune*, warned that by some such combination of accident and ineptitude as this our world might end sooner rather than later, unless it disarmed itself.

Meanwhile, back in the fifties, the list of the things he was against continued to grow and to be reflected ever increasingly in the headlines. He was against the pools, and the suicide of a Methodist choirmaster, who had been asked to resign after winning £700 in one, gave Donald his cue. 'Let us clear our minds of sentimentality. The fact that the man committed suicide only adds an emotional touch to the story, but does not invalidate it, or corroborate the main factors from the Christian point of view. It is not a condition of membership of the Methodist Church that you should refrain from gambling; but it is an understood thing that a Methodist does not gamble. In my judgement, gambling for the Christian is impermissible.' He was against capital punishment, and here again a contemporary event, the execution of Ruth Ellis, the last woman, as it turned out, to hang in Britain, set him off. 'It would be degrading, retrograde and un-Christian to hang Ruth Ellis', Dr Soper told a lunchtime crowd in Manchester, 'Two Royal Commissions have protested against the iniquity of capital punishment. I believe that there is no person, male or female, sufficiently bad to be written off as a loss to the community.' He condemned conditions in Hola Camp, a detention centre for Mau Mau prisoners in Kenya during the disturbances there, where several prisoners had died. He was against Dr Kinsey, that now almost-forgotten sexologist who caused something of a sensation in 1953 with his book, *The Sexual Behaviour of the American Male*. 'The reasons why people are interested in Dr Kinsey's book are unworthy. They are not interested in science, but enjoy the pornographic material they hope to find in the book. I wish he had spent his time more profitably.' He was, as always, against armaments of any kind. 'The Way to the Cross is not the way of the guided missile.' He was against premium bonds, on their introduction in 1956. 'Any Government that takes gambling into its system is politically bankrupt.' He was against Moral Rearmament. 'It is important that the idea should not get abroad that the Free Churches as a whole are behind the Moral Rearmament campaign. As President of the Methodist Conference I do not believe that the Moral Rearmament programme is in the best interests of the Kingdom of Heaven.' He was, however, in favour of betting shops, telling the Church's Committee on Gambling in 1956 that he believed that 'it would be better for us not to oppose the betting shops than to persist in what appears to our fellows as a thorough piece of hypocrisy. Rigid control of betting shops would be better than the flaunting of vice, lawbreaking, the temptation of the police and the sense of profound injustice felt by members of the community.'

On another kind of issue altogether, he defended the BBC's action, in 1955, in allowing a humanist, Mrs Margaret Knight, to broadcast in a series on 'Morals without Religion', talks critical of Christianity. The affair, which would pass quite unremarked now, created something of an uproar at the time. Donald was prompt with comment. 'I am appalled at the working of hysteria on what seems to be a matter of normal procedure on the part of the BBC in giving a measure of freedom in religious disagreement, as it does on other issues. Christians will do themselves a great deal of harm if they assume that the Christian faith is a kind of hothouse plant that needs to be protected against the weather.'

There were three issues which in particular brought Donald, in these years, not only into the headlines, but into trouble. The first, which, like Mrs Knight's broadcast, would pass unremarked today, arose out of his criticism for the Queen's fondness for horseracing. Speaking outdoors in Deansgate, Manchester, in November 1953, he said: 'I wish the Queen did not go to horse races. She would be very much wiser if she kept away from the sport of kings. It is very obviously a household of racketeers. You know it, and I know it.' He said it again in Edinburgh two days later. All kinds of peculiar results followed. The *Daily Mirror* said that this President of the Methodist Conference ought to explain himself to Sir Humphrey de Trafford, Major-General Sir Randle Feilden and the Duke of Norfolk, stewards of the Jockey Club. Maybe they would want to suspend Dr Soper's licence to ride his hobby horse until he thought over what he was talking about. The civic reception for Donald in Berwick-on-Tweed was called off by an indignant mayor. When Donald did go there the town hall was closed to him and he addressed the crowd from the steps. At Kingsway Hall, various people withheld contributions to the customary Christmas funds. An Australian paper accused him of nagging the Throne. Even the *Methodist Recorder* thought it regrettable that he should wag his admonitory finger, as it put it, at the Royal Family, and, at a place called Bedlington and Wallington, the General Purposes Committee refused him the use of a public park for a meeting. What the persons more personally concerned with the matter thought about it, if anything, is not on record. But years later Donald became the first Methodist minister to preach at Sandringham.

The second issue which excited opinion followed hard upon this one. Speaking at Cambridge, and while still President, he said: 'We are in many ways an occupied country, and we are certainly the junior partner in the alliance with America. When I read that the Americans are starting to build schools, I say it does look as if they are here permanently. America today is pursuing power politics quite ruthlessly.' Asked if he would like to see the Russians here, he replied: 'Yes, very much. Most of them are quite decent fellows. We have got the Americans here, so let's have the Russians as well. Anyway, who said the Russians want to invade anywhere?' Such remarks could not but be wildly provocative, and when in the following year, 1954, it became known that Donald intended to visit Russia, which he duly did, the fact was regarded by some with dark suspicion. He was much heckled about it before a crowd of two thousand in Market Square, Nottingham, during the course of a visit there, and his famous remark, made at an earlier Methodist Conference, that he would not resist if the Russians invaded, was once more brought out and used in evidence against him. He was not in the least put out, and two years later, when Bulganin and Khruschev visited London, he wrote to invite them to attend Evening Service at Kingsway Hall.

The third considerable controversy of his Presidential year came out of Donald's disapproval of Billy Graham. Arising at the height of the American evangelist's power and influence, in the same year as his mission campaign based on Harringay, this aroused much feeling, especially as many Methodist churches had sent parties there to hear Graham. Donald, speaking in the Wimborne circuit shortly afterwards, told them bluntly that the money they had been paying to get to Harringay should have been given to their own churches. Before the Grand Campaign began, however, he had already attacked the whole concept behind it, describing some passages in a book of Billy Graham's as intellectual rubbish and emotional escapism. He said he felt it was all the sadder because this kind of thing would only encourage 'those who in other circumstances would turn to the Christian faith, to turn to something which they feel will do more credit to their minds'. He added, 'I am certain that Christian truth passes our understanding. I am equally sure that it never by-passes it.'

. . . .

Donald carried his controversy-causing capacity abroad with him when, after the war, he resumed his overseas travels. These were most extensive and took him the world over. Indeed, in 1952 he went round the world. It would be easy to gain the impression, from the records of these journeys as reflected in headlines from Vancouver to Tokio, that here was a traveller who attracted sharp press comment as a magnet attracts pins. There is truth in that. But the facts should not be allowed to obscure the further fact that here was a man 'doing the work of an evangelist', with all the strength that he had and at a killing pace. So it was news when he told Americans, surely not without truth, that they were 'needlessly frightened by Reds'; but not news that his purpose in being on that side of the Atlantic at all was to speak at missions and conventions both in the United States and Canada. There was a mission, for example, in Vancouver which packed the cathedral for the opening service, did the same on the second evening in the largest Free Church in the city, and on the third evening crowded 2,800 people into a public hall. This led to the setting-up of a branch of the Order of Christian Witness in Vancouver, the first of its kind in Canada. It was news when, going straight on to Australia, he got into trouble with the Prime Minister of that country, who rebuked him for saying he would vote 'no' if he had been qualified to do so, in a referendum then being held in Australia on whether Communism should be banned. Mr Menzies was indignant, saying he had read about 'a reverend gentleman who had arrived in the country and in one hour had mastered the Constitution, the Statute Law of the Commonwealth, and a full knowledge of Australian circumstances. He must be brilliant, if conceited, a man to learn that lot in an hour', said the Prime Minister. 'I have devoted twenty years of my life to learning them.'

But it was not news that, on the same visit, 2,000 people listened to Donald on two Sundays in the Domain, Sydney's Hyde Park; 1,500 on the Yarra River bank in Melbourne; another 2,000 outside Brisbane Town Hall, 4,000 at a rally in Elder Park, Adelaide, and 800 on two successive Sundays on the Esplanade at Perth. Or that he spoke in many of the places where men worked, on the wharves, in iron foundries and railway works.

It was certainly news when Alexei, Patriarch of Moscow and All Russia, invited him there in 1954 as part of a delegation which included Canon Raven, former Vice-Chancellor of Cambridge, and a pacifist colleague of Donald's in former days, to visit Russia. But it was a smaller story, apparently, when Donald told nearly two thousand Russians in Moscow's Baptist Church that this visiting delegation of British church leaders brought 'not only our love, but also that of many Christians who are worshipping in England today'. The congregation replied in unison, 'We thank you'.

And so it went on. He was in the West Indies in 1954, New Zealand the following year, preaching and speaking for a month. It was on his return from this particularly arduous effort that he cracked. One symption of the crack was persistent insomnia, a disorder from which he never recovered, never has, and which he had even by that date endured in silence for a long time. He was ordered on this occasion to get away for three months from his London commitments. He therefore went to Poland, a country to which Methodism had found its way in 1920, at the invitation of the Methodist Church in Warsaw. He was there for thirteen days, returning with his customary headline-making statement. 'I believe that Poland stands in a unique position within the Communist world. Rejection of the evil elements in Stalinism began there earlier than anywhere else. I have, too, been much impressed by the signs of material improvement.'

The next year it was Japan, for a month's campaign in September to celebrate one hundred years of Protestant Christian missionary effort there. Hiroshima, from so passionate a pacifist as Donald, was bound to trigger off strong reaction. 'It is a symbol of the futility and the curse of war itself. That curse is seen in every Japanese city, and seeps through the conversation of every Japanese who can be persuaded to do more than bow to you, and drink tea with you. That futility is manifest in the almost automatic reproduction of the city with a rabbit-like fecundity.' But this visit to Japan also drew from him one of those oddly prophetic statements which he made from time to time. 'Tokio today has risen from the ashes of the city which was largely burnt to the ground. It is the creation of modern, scientific, industralised, secular man, with its functional business houses and factories. It is a staggering comment on his sheer ability to produce the apparatus he needs for the economic life he desires. It is this industrial fecundity which I find so frightening, even more so than the human fecundity of a people which now numbers ninety million and makes a huge addition to this total each new year. I wonder whether this frenzied, buzzing new Japan is doomed to produce nothing but warrior bees to defend a dying hive. It seems to me the sort of bush-fire capitalism that threatens to curse the future even more terribly than it has cursed the past.'

Such were some of the travels of these years, costly in physical and nervous effort, and often, because of their controversial by-products and open-air confrontations, rough passages very different from the smoother progresses of other Christian notables. And always, awaiting his return, was the continuing work of the West London Mission at the Kingsway Hall. 1957 saw the twenty-first anniversary of his Superintendency. It was to continue to be the home base of his ministry; the place from which he went out to travel various and distinct paths in public life. Down one of those paths, which may be called the way to Socialism, we can now follow him.

5

# The Road to Socialism

It is not in my judgement possible to be a practising Christian today without having a clear idea as to how Christianity is politically interpreted.

D.O.S. in 'Frankly Speaking', BBC programme (29.7.65)

I have never found in the history of the Church that there has been anything like the rumpus when the Church has committed itself to the Right, as there is when members of the Church like myself commit themselves to the Left.

Ibid.

The only other person I have known in politics who would so persistently seek to apply first principles to the situation was Aneurin Bevan.

Michael Foot, MP

I think he is in a long and very great tradition of clerics who have played a part in what used to be called, in Victorian times, 'the condition of England question.'

The Right Hon. Harold Wilson, MP

'THOSE WHO tell the Church to keep out of politics are talking nonsense. If politics is the way in which we conduct everyday affairs, then politics is a proper way in which we are to seek the Kingdom of God.' Delegates to the Labour Party's Annual Conference of 1953, the year of Donald's Presidency, heard him say this in St Stephen's Methodist Church, Cliftonville, at the Sunday morning service which, traditionally, opened the week. James Griffiths read a first Lesson in which the prophet Micah looked to a time when swords would be beaten into ploughshares. Clement Attlee read the second Lesson. Delegates packed the building. None of them was likely to have been much surprised to hear Donald go on to say that he would resist the temptation to give them good advice, however much he may feel they needed it. Before anyone had a right to offer good advice in the name of Christ it was necessary to work for the establishment of foundations on which faith could be built. There must be economic and political action before the kingdom of this world could be made into the Kingdom of God.

They would not have been surprised because this was the Donald Soper familiar to so many, a man pursuing the road to Socialism with something of the earnestness and urgency with which Christian in *Pilgrim's Progress* took the track from the City of Destruction to a better place. This high moral motivation behind Donald's politics makes it, strictly speaking, inaccurate to refer to his Socialism as one of the several paths he has travelled through life, as though it were distinct from the others. For him, Socialism, like pacifism, has been an essential element in his Christianity, and has to be seen as such if anything of its true nature, especially its insistence upon principles and impatience with compromise, is to be understood. The necessity for Socialism, in the sense of social justice, seems to have come upon him in a moment of time, with the force of a revelation. The place was a railway works at Derby, visited during a mission in the early twenties. He had never before encountered industry or the lives of those who work in it, and here he was confronted with the harsh realities of industrial life as they were then. He said once in a broadcast that he went in at one end of those works politically uncommitted, and came out at the other end a Socialist, presumably meaning by this that he saw in the conditions there revealed a degree of social injustice which he felt was intolerable, and for which he felt it was worth while working to eradicate. The surprise felt by him can be compared with the effect upon him of the discovery of poverty in south London in the early years of his ministry.

These origins are important in that they clearly conditioned his Socialism into what has always been essentially a part of the politics of protest, born in him in the lean years of the twenties and thirties. So there have always been for him wrongs to be righted, battles to be fought, enemies—especially capitalist enemies—to be overcome, principles upheld, and in general a better world created through political action motivated by the highest moral principles. This classic posture of the political purist can obviously be more readily maintained in opposition than in power. Power brings responsibilities and the need for compromise which usually accompanies them. So Donald's Socialism, like that of so many of his generation who came to political consciousness when the Labour Party was a force outside the walls of the capitalist establishment, has always been for him a cause rather than just a manifestation of politics as the art of the possible. The position obviously changes when the besiegers outside, through electoral victory, enter the fortress and become themselves for a time the Establishment, as the government of the day. When that happens, their more doctrinaire supporters tend to become somewhat more isolated figures, even if much admired.

Something of the sort could certainly be said to have happened to Donald. A conscience-stirring influence in British Socialism for a long time, he has often been a severe critic of its political expression. He has had his enemies; he has made his friends. One of the most distinguished of the latter, Harold Wilson, Prime Minister from 1964 to 1970, said of Donald, 'He is the sort of man you feel you've always known. I met him a number of times at meetings linking the Church with the Party, and as he was living near me I had a number of talks with him about that, and got to know him. I suppose the next time I was in direct contact with him was in 1962 to celebrate the Festival of Labour in Battersea Gardens (I was Chairman of the Party at that time). He conducted the service. In the government of 1964 I decided as soon as the House met for the Queen's Speech—I think it was the morning before or the morning after—to have a service in the Crypt Chapel of the House of Commons. The service was conducted then, and again in 1966, in a new government, by Donald Soper.' The first of these Crypt Chapel services was in fact noted by the Press. 'One of the less noticed and more tranquil parliamentary events of the week', wrote the *Daily Telegraph*, 'has been a religious service in the Crypt for members of Mr Wilson's Administration. He read from St Matthew's Gospel, Dr Soper led prayers, Dr Stockwood, Bishop of Southwark, preached the sermon. In their Act of Dedication, Ministers used these words: "With God's help we will try to be his faithful servants. We will be honest in our thinking, fair in our judgement and generous towards those who differ. We will strive to live in love and charity with all men." '

'In 1966', Mr Wilson added, 'we were all impressed by a tremendous prayer of dedication Donald Soper used, and I said afterwards that I was going to use that prayer at the end of the Parliament on a television broadcast. In the event I didn't. But I did conclude one of my Party Conference speeches with the whole text.[1] I also remember one of the greatest sermons I've ever heard. We always have a Conference Service before Conference begins. It was, I think, in Brighton about eight years ago that he preached. Everyone said that if there was a single speech from the platform half as good, or half as eloquent, or half as Socialist as that, it would be a good Conference.'

The ideological basis for Donald's Socialism seems remarkably

[1] The text of the prayer was:

> O God, grant us a vision of our land, fair as it might be
> A land of righteousness where none shall wrong his neighbour;
> A land of plenty where evil and poverty shall be done away;
> A land of brotherhood where all success shall be founded on
> service, and honour shall be given on excellence alone;
> A land of peace, where order shall not rest on force, but on
> the love of all for the common life and weal;
> Bless our efforts to make the vision a living reality;
> Inspire and strengthen each one of us that we may give time.
> thought, and sacrifice to speed the day of its coming.

Mr Wilson added: 'When the time comes, I would want this Government, this Movement, to be judged not only by the British nation, but by history, by our success or failure in turning this prayer into a reality.'

simple when exhibited unadorned. Thus, asked for the rationale of it, he said: 'You cannot, it seems to me, follow Jesus Christ unless you accept his teaching, as well as seek to be inspired by his spirit. And the teaching of Jesus Christ seems to me to be inevitably linked with Socialism. The argument would go something like this, that we believe that a fuller understanding of the Christian faith came to the disciples at the time of Pentecost, when suddenly it lighted up. And we know what they did. They set up a Socialist community. Now you can say if you like that this was a mistake. But it is theologically difficult to say that the first thing these people did under the inspiration of the Holy Spirit was to make a mistake. I don't think they made a mistake at all. I think it's we who have been making a mistake ever since. And the rationale of the Socialist argument is that, in fact, this is what the Christians did under the first inspiration of the teaching of their Lord.'

He developed this in a broadcast interview with St John Stevas in 1965. 'The foundation of my Socialist belief is that I regard Socialism as the economic and political expression, in time, of what I believe to be the Kingdom of God. But I would never try to put a quart into a pint pot, and I am very well aware that there is much more in Christianity than in Socialism. But for me, Socialism is the extension of the teaching of our Lord, so that it covers the whole of human existence. For me, Clause 4[1] expresses, within the framework of a contemporary economic situation, what I believe to be the ultimate principle that emerges from our Lord's teaching, that this world ought to be conceived as a home, the goods of the world ought to be set on a family table, that a chair ought to be provided for members of that family, and what they need should not be provided for them according to their ability to pay for it, but because it belongs to

[1] 'To secure for the workers, by hand or by brain, the full fruits of their industry and the most equitable distribution thereof, that may be possible, upon the basis of the common ownership of the means of production, distribution, and exchange, and the best obtainable system of popular administration and control of each industry or service.' *Labour Party Constitution of 1918*.

them. I believe that everybody has an inalienable right to food, clothing and shelter, whether they be good, bad or indifferent.'

This basic simplicity of Donald's political motivation, unchanged over the years, gives place to a much greater sophistication when it comes to their application to specific issues and situations. The statement that deeds count more than words is not true of the politician. The opposite applies. So Donald's contribution to Socialism in his time is to be measured, in the first place, by what he said, as a Christian Socialist spokesman. In season and out of season—usually the latter, judging by the reactions, ranging from indignation to fury, which his statements have touched off—he has spoken out on what he has seen as the truth. This has usually been expressed in highly critical terms.

'Why doesn't the Pope intervene?' he was asking way back in the time of the Spanish Civil War. The Church—this time the Church in general—had no right to leave it to the Left Wing to translate into practical terms the Christian way of life, he was telling a huge gathering in the north in 1950. As so often, he was fiercely attacked in the questions which followed and, as usual, fought back. 'You have no right to leave these matters as if they did not count. If you do leave them, you must not complain if the Communists take them up.' The United Nations was all very well, he was saying in the immediate post-war years when that body had just risen from the ashes, but world government without nation states was the only realistic hope for mankind. The United States, let alone the United Nations, often drew his fire. We should get out of Korea, he was saying, when Britain was at war in that country. For that matter, the United States should get out of Britain, which was, he was saying in 1952, being turned into an advance air base for the United States Air Force. This was at the Durham Methodist Big Meeting. The Durham miners gala around the same time was a tougher proposition: few were disposed to be interested in Donald, having been stunned by Aneurin Bevan earlier on. But Donald drew a large crowd when, having taken off his jacket, denounced Dr Malan of South

Africa, the Conservative government at home, asked why, if only the weak-kneed went to church, as was popularly supposed, the strong-kneed should therefore stay at home, he expressed a wish that more people in the Labour Party were Socialists. This was when he was President of Conference. Colonialism was wrong at all times, in all places, and in every respect he said at an open-air meeting in Huntingdon in the same year. 'The idea that a particular group of people can own and control others in perpetuity is anti-Christian.' The armed services should be done away with. This was at Devonport. When the Mau Mau in Kenya were active, he advocated a complete withdrawal of white settlers. At the Oxford Union he was victorious in a tremendous debate with Oleg Kerensky, grandson of the last Prime Minister of Russia, on the motion 'This house refuses to be frightened by the Communist bogey'.

The deportation of Archbishop Makarios from Cyprus was a mortal error in 1956. There was a lot of good in Nasser, he asserted, when the Suez crisis was building up. He should not be repressed. When the attempt was made to do so, Donald denounced it and led a protest procession of his Kingsway congregation through London's West End, wearing—not carrying—a banner with the strange device, 'Stop Gunboat Diplomacy'. In 1961 he protested so hard against the Immigration Bill at a meeting in St Pancras Town Hall that the platform was attacked and a free fight ensued.

Of course such views and such conduct were bound to bring reactions. Sometimes they came—the unkindest cut of all—from some of the very people whose side he was on, like the secretary of the North Staffordshire Women's Advisory Council of the Labour Party, who criticised him in the Press for mixing politics with religion. 'As a politician, he would be a great leader. As a minister of religion, he is one. But it is a grave wrong to attempt to be both.' Sometimes, and more often, criticisms came from members of his own Church. An example was a letter from prominent Methodists in the mid-Bedfordshire Division, who expressed 'strong repugnance' when Donald wrote in support of the Socialist candidate, Mr Skeffington-Lodge, in the election of 1953. 'We feel sure that our fellow Nonconformists will share our repugnance at the suggestion, in the letter, that Socialists have a monopoly of the Christian virtues.'

Such reactions certainly witnessed to the truth of Donald's remark that church history showed that there was usually far sharper reaction when some member of it committed himself to the Left, than when some member committed himself to the Right. This kind of criticism also exhibited the ignorance, widespread but always surprising, of the fact that there has been a long tradition of Christian involvement, not only with politics, but with radical politics, sometimes of a revolutionary nature. John Ball, implicated in the fourteenth-century insurrection of Wat Tyler and executed for it, was, after all, a priest. Langland's *Piers Plowman* is both political and imflammatory in parts. Wycliffe's ideas of private property were radical. Charles Kingsley said he was a Chartist. So many clergy spoke for the Labour candidate in the Jarrow by-election of 1907 that an old miner came out of an election meeting exclaiming, 'It's like being in church'. William Temple in his day gravely disturbed the belief that Archbishops of Canterbury were necessarily a part of the economic establishment. There have existed for a long time, moreover, a number of associations of people consciously both Christian and Socialist. Two of them with whom Donald has been involved were the Union of Socialist Christian Ministers and Clergy, and the Christian Socialist Crusade. Some ten years ago a gathering of these met at the Lamb public house, in London, and produced a document called 'Letters from the Lamb' in which they advocated the revival of, and showed their anxiety about the future of, Christianity and Socialism. Donald was drawn into this with the Bishop of Southwark, Mervyn Stockwood, and John Groser, a celebrated East End Anglican priest, later Master of the Royal Foundation of St Katherine's, together with Tom Driberg and others. A mass meeting was held in the

Kingsway Hall to revive the Christian Socialist movement in general. Out of this meeting, which was, incidentally, one of the very last attended by the redoubtable R. H. Tawney, author of *Religion and the Rise of Capitalism,* sprang at least an attempt to revive the Christian Socialist Movement. This reached back in its origins to the Christian Social Union, founded by Henry Scott Holland and Charles Gore in 1889, to the Guild of St Matthew's, creation of Stuart Headlam, rector of St Matthews in Bethnal Green before that, and to the thinking of such men as Ludlow and F. D. Maurice earlier still.

Donald, at the Kingsway Hall meeting, was elected Chairman of the Christian Socialist Movement and has held that office ever since. Harold Wilson recently addressed a meeting of it. So Donald has been by no means alone in his politics, nor in the disapproval which his combination of them with his religion has occasioned. In fact, he has not combined them so much as seen them as essentially one. To be attacked upon the propriety of mixing religion with politics is, however, only one of the occupational hazards to which a man who does so is subject. Another, if he happens to be a Socialist, is to be asked whether he thinks it necessary to be of that persuasion in order to be a Christian. It is, of course, a well-worn question. Donald's answer, none the less, might surprise some by its tolerance and moderation. He said, 'I am not disposed to lay down a general rule about it, because the word Christian involves so many varying interpretations. If by a Christian you mean one who is honestly and sincerely endeavouring to be a disciple of Jesus Christ, then I must find room in my Christianity for those who may radically disagree with me on political and economic issues. On the other hand I must say, and feel, that they are lacking, I believe, in a perception of what the Christian faith really is. Another way of answering the question would be to say this; that in the end, as a final Christian commitment, I am perfectly certain that Socialism is implicit and cannot be disregarded and cannot be left out.'

When Aneurin Bevan in 1955 made one of his less fortunate remarks to the effect that Conservatism was inconsistent with Christianity, Donald agreed with him but felt bound to add that, even so, he felt there were many Conservatives who were better Christians than many Socialists.

Donald's association with this remarkable Welshman, Member for Ebbw Vale, Minister of Health in the Attlee government, then Minister of Labour and National Service until his resignation, ended on a hill top at Waun Pound in the centre of Bevan's constituency, near his home town of Tredegar on 15 July 1960. The occasion was an open-air memorial service for Nye Bevan, who had died a week previously. For Donald, the bleak, cold mountainside, where for forty years Bevan had addressed meetings, the crowd of 5,000, the hymns, the intense emotion, remained a very vivid memory. He was proud to have been asked to conduct the service. He said: 'I knew Aneurin Bevan fairly well. I spoke with him on a number of platforms and admired his technique and his beautiful voice, and his command of expressive, evocative language. I found him a great figure, and I can remember now the consummate ease with which he dealt with hecklers, and the lyrical turn which his oratory possessed. I regarded Bevan as a man of outstanding quality. I don't know how deep and profound was his religious conviction.' Nor did the rest of the world, for that matter, in which the dead man had been by no means universally popular. As his crematorium ceremony in London had been prayerless, it had drawn unworthy taunts of atheism. This, according to Mr John Beecham, a London physiotherapist and a close friend of Bevan's, was quite untrue. 'Churchmen like Donald Soper and the Bishop of Southwark were among his friends. He admired them greatly.' So Donald had the honour of conducting this memorial service. It was not an easy thing to do. But it did enable him to pay a tribute he felt was needed. 'I salute a man who was good in the essential sense of that word.' It did enable him to help the widow, Jennie Lee, to say her word, too. Donald led her to the microphone, where she spoke into an utter silence, followed when she finished by tremendous applause. One of those present, in addition to Michael Foot, was Jim Callaghan, years later to be Home Secretary in the Wilson government. Once, when a Customs clerk in the City of London, he had been for a long time one of Donald's front-rank listeners on Tower Hill. 'As regular as clockwork', Donald said, 'I can see now the string-bean of a fellow. He reminds me of it when he sees me. He was one of my boys on Tower Hill.'

Such were some of Donald's contacts with Labour Party personalities. There were others. 'I heard Hugh Dalton—if you were within a mile of him when he was speaking you couldn't avoid hearing him. Stafford Cripps was a figurehead to me, a man of austere morality. Clement Attlee, who once invited me to preach the sermon at a Labour Party Conference, was almost an anonymous figure, in the sense that you did not come away with any sense of personality. He was the very opposite of that. But I thought that he was a man of deep conviction and very great consistency—one who was almost entirely free from the things which haunt and vex most of us human beings—envy and malice and pride and jealousy. He was a man alone, and very largely a man for others, I thought. Harold Wilson is the most relaxed man I have ever met in my life. He is of piercing intelligence within the contours of those things which he has made his own, and in which he is interested. He is sincere and genuine, and as far as my own contacts with him have gone, he has always been invariably kind and reasonable.'

None of these personal cordialities, however, have prevented Donald from being a severe critic of his own party from time to time. 'No Socialist government in my time has fully professed, in its actions, the kind of total Socialism which would be included in Clause 4 of the Manifesto. I think this is because many people joined the party who were not committed Socialists by any means. They are people who were anxious to get rid of what they believed to be a bad administration, but were by no means committed to the all-out interpretation of Socialism. And that is why, from time to time, within the Labour Party, there have been the Left Wingers who have been trying to bring the Party as a whole to the Socialism to which, officially, it has never been attached. The Wilson administration is a case in point. Wilson endeavoured to get a consensus by appealing to the middle classes, and by equating his programme with a mixed economy and seeking to do most of the changes towards social justice by fiscal rather than by revolutionary or political means. Looking back, I think it was a gamble which failed and I would think that, had the Wilson administration gone all out for a much more Socialist commitment they might have had greater success. This is a harsh judgement, and we are all to blame to a certain extent. But I hope that we have learned from it that a Labour Party which is not Socialist is a contradiction in terms, and more or less a waste of time.'

The area of Donald's political activity has been wide. A speaker on Left-wing platforms for years, dating back to his Islington days when he supported Leah Manning as candidate, he has been a public figure on Tower Hill and in Hyde Park long enough to have become a part of the scene usually dominated by political themes. He has written, he has preached his political creed, he has given concrete expression to it in the social work at the West London Mission. He is a member of the parliamentary Labour Party. And he has marched, figuratively and often literally, with many of those armies of protest which have passed, under various banners, across the public arena long enough for some of those involved when young to have become middle-aged.

An important and clearly definable area of political activity for him was the London County Council, of which Donald was made an Alderman in 1958. The fact alone is a tribute to the extent of his specialist knowledge in such fields of social work as had been carried out under him at the West London Mission. The LCC had a tradition of bringing in, not by election but by nomination, people from outside whose experience could be of value to it. This happened to Donald, to the surprise of some, because he had no previous identification with the Council. Lady Serota, now a colleague of Donald's in the House of Lords, and chairman of the LCC Children's Committee on which he served for some years, said that 'When Donald became a member of the LCC there were certain groups within the Labour group who were very suspicious of him. He carried the pacifist label, quite apart from the fact that he was a minister of religion, plus the fact that he holds views that were regarded as being on the extreme Left of the Party. He was never expelled from the Labour group—we wouldn't have that. But he was not popular in all quarters.'

He may not have been expelled; but his difference with the then Labour establishment on the LCC in 1959 was of a serious order and arose out of a fundamental issue of freedom of speech and comment. The Party that year had a mammoth majority, the largest in its history. Soon afterwards it ruled that: 'No member shall write to the Press or make public statements either orally or in writing, attacking the policy of the Party in the decisions of the group. In the event of any violation of this rule, a member, or members, render themselves liable to the Whip being withdrawn. This was altogether too much for Donald. 'Stephen Leacock once said', he wrote in *Tribune*, ' "Never take the bull by the horns unless it is absolutely necessary. But if it is, then do it at once before the bull gets round to the idea and tries to get away." I propose to take this advice with regard to the recent decision of the Labour group in the LCC.' He then assailed the whole thing. 'I publicly criticise, attack, repudiate, denounce, execrate and abominate it, and I hope these words taken together will give an unambiguous impression of where I stand in the matter.' He then went on to say, at length and in detail, exactly why.

So violent a cannonade might have been expected to draw counter-fire. In fact, nothing happened, and at a subsequent meeting of the Council a Conservative member asked the chairman of the Establishments Committee why a copy of

*Tribune*, containing at attack on the ban, was missing from the members' Reading Room. That, he was told, was a matter for speculation.

It was a famous victory; but it did not help Donald to make friends, even if it enabled him to influence people. There was certainly, in Lady Serota's view, a personality clash between him and Sir Isaac Hayward, the leader of the Labour group. But 'they learned to live together, two great individualists, and in their own way remarkable people, but bitterly opposed in terms of their belief'.

Without a doubt, Donald could be awkward. He embarrassed his own party on several occasions at County Hall, notably on issues involving Civil Defence, which he considered a waste of time short of complete nuclear disarmament. But these were only incidents in a long term of service on the LCC and GLC.

Yet another platform for Donald's politics has been the independent Socialist weekly, *Tribune*. This paper, a hard-hitting publication in a long tradition of radical journalism was founded in 1937, and has had some notable editors, H. J. Hartshorn, Raymond Postgate, Aneurin Bevan, Michael Foot, Richard Clements. How a Methodist minister came to be a regular contributor is an interesting story. Michael Foot, MP, Managing Director of the paper, told it frankly. 'The first time I ever heard his name was when my mother, who was a very strong Methodist, and knew that my opinions were very much on the Left, and who was dubious about my Methodism, said that the person I really ought to meet was Donald Soper. That was years before I had met him. He did an occasional article for us on *Tribune*. Then I went round with Bob Edwards, who was the editor at that time, to ask him to do us a regular column. These contributions he has sustained in an amazing way over a long period. Of course, he has had many critics among *Tribune*'s agnostic, or atheist, or anti-religious readers. Some of them are angered by what he writes; but many of them, I believe, see the virtue of the way in which he says things, and the importance for Socialists that he should say them. He is the outstanding representative of Christian Socialism in this country. So we were very proud and pleased to have him writing so persistently for *Tribune*. He did it as an astonishing self-sacrifice, because he would take a great deal of trouble in writing the articles. He would consult with us very often about the subjects. He would be extremely forthcoming in the way in which he was prepared to do the subject that we thought would be most helpful at a particular time, and all this without his receiving a penny piece, and therefore the amount of time that he has given in an extremely busy life is something beyond praise as far as we are concerned.'

Some of these articles, always appearing under the heading 'Personally Speaking', exhibit as the years pass, that element of the prophetic which keeps occurring in Donald's utterances. It has now become, for instance, a widespread American and, indeed, world anxiety that there is something seriously wrong with the state of that country's society. Donald was saying this in *Tribune* when the world was agape with astonished admiration at the latest moon-shots. 'The space paraphernalia of Houston, and the enormous expenditure of the space programme are beginning to be seen in stark contrast to the neglected Skid Rows, the appalling slums of New York and Chicago, and the sheer poverty of public welfare in many States.'

This prophetic element is so remarkable as to warrant a closer look in a wider context. Any man who, like Donald, has been saying so often for so many years that so much was wrong with human affairs can easily draw the same reactions as did the prophet Jeremiah, and the indignation aroused tends to increase in proportion as he turns out to be right. In the end there will be naught for his comfort as well as little for anybody else, for the world does not relish those who tell it that it is going, with ever-increasing rapidity, the wrong way. And Donald has been doing just this. It might have seemed inopportune to say, at the creation of the United Nations, that world government was the only realistic hope for the future. But who would deny it now, even while despairing of its feasibility? And if colonialism was wrong in 1953, as he averred, it has vanished by now, only to reappear in Russian and American reincarnations. The deportation of Markarios in 1956 was an error. We can see it now. Donald saw it then. His Beatitude is now President of Cyprus. It was infuriating, no doubt, to say at the time of Suez that there was a lot of good in Nasser. But the world, having since then seen the funeral of that personage with its extraordinary upburst of his country's affection, may well wonder whether there was not, after all, something in what Donald said. And as for the iniquity of clergymen being involved in politics, who is startled now when an Anglican Dean in South Africa is arrested under an anti-terrorism measure, or when two Roman Catholic priests go to jail in the United States for opposing the Vietnam War? All these things happened in 1971.

In any event, the road to Socialism for Donald, with its starting point in the sincere belief that the Kingdom of God could be furthered through political views, and its subsequent passage through the heavily mined deserts of a fearful stretch of history, has not been easy whatever else it has been. Whether it has been necessary or even whether democratic Socialism, as he and his generation saw it, is any longer a viable goal in the modern world, with it infinite complexities of organisation, are other questions, and very important ones. As to the first, some words which have been recently written about another Left-wing cleric, John Groser, are relevant. 'It may well be that the enemy will not be the oppressive Capitalism of old; it may well be that old ghosts such as the means test and mass unemployment have been buried for ever. But the depersonalising of society has certainly not been buried as a possibility. Nor has the danger of some totalitarian takeover of an economically failing society, such as is our own today.'[1]

As to the second, who can say? Revolution rather than evolution, violence more than reasoned argument, seem now to

[1] *John Groser, East London Priest,* edited by Kenneth Brill (Mowbrays, 1971).

express the mood of some who seek, however undesirably, social change along those lines. And Donald himself has ex pressed a sense of the current decay of the older Socialist faith which has motivated him. Writing in *Tribune* in March 1971 he said; 'The general setting is one of religious and political agnosticism. Not a few did believe and still believe in the practicability of the Kingdom of God on earth. None the less, that sort of faith has gravely diminished and with its going has also gone its political partner, the secular conviction that we are moving scientifically and predictably into the earthly paradise of Socialism.'

That may indeed well be so. But of the quality, as well as the steadfastness and courage of his own loyality to this ideal, there can be no doubt. Michael Foot summed it up: 'I think that he has been an extremely good influence on the whole of the political outlook of the Labour movement. He is advocating the fundamental change which a Socialist society would involve, outlining how radical are the changes in men's outlook which must be involved if a proper Socialist society is to be built. The danger of the Labour movement all through these years has been that it would be too pragmatist and empirical, and he is perpetually calling it to first principles.' Meanwhile, and for him, leading off this road to Socialism, there has been another route which Donald has found it necessary to travel—the road to Aldermaston.

# 6

# The Road to Aldermaston

I am thoroughly in favour of umbrellas, for I think they have done more in the last few months than battleships could have done.

D.O.S. on Tower Hill, following the Munich Agreement of 29 September 1938

Look at how much of his own moral codes man has to break to keep his spirit in being by war. He defeats his own ends. One of the things that I accept is that evil can only be overcome by good. We have enough historical evidence to show that the overthrow of violence produces more violence.

D.O.S. in *Picture Post*, 5 August 1950

What is the difference between putting a baby on the fire and putting the fire on the baby? Surely, the answer is, the anonymity of 25,000 feet.

D.O.S. in Defence Estimates debate, House of Lords, 8 March 1966

Manpower dosen't matter now. Somebody's got a few men with buttons to press.

D.O.S. speaking in 1970

IN THE early thirties, an oddly assorted group set off from Central London for Tilbury, there to take ship, they hoped, for the Far East, where at that time Japan and China were at war. They were, in alphabetical order, Brigadier-General F. P. Crozier, the Reverend Doctor Herbert Gray, the Reverend Maude Royden, Canon H. R. L. Sheppard and Donald Soper. Their collective intention was to place themselves between the belligerents at a place called Chopei, where much blood was currently being shed. In the event, the five never got beyond the docks, although their manifestly good intentions aroused some sympathy. So Donald remembered the incident. Asked what in fact on that distant day they actually expected to accomplish, he replied: 'To tell you the truth I don't know. But we were enthusiastically following the leadership of Dick Sheppard and he had a number of ideas. I'm not sure that he'd thought them out particularly carefully. But we felt unless we could raise a sufficient army to go to Chopei it wouldn't be much good, and we didn't get enough recruits by any means. We had a good deal of opposition, but we started demonstrations and meetings. I can remember one very big one in the Albert Hall, when Charles Raven, Vice-Chancellor of Cambridge University, took the chair. We had meetings up and down the country. We had one tremendous affair, which I shall never forget, at Dorchester, with Vera Brittain, George Lansbury, Dick Sheppard and myself as the principal speakers. This was really comparable with the best days of the CND in public response.'

But that little journey to Tilbury has more significance at this point than a report of any of the mass meetings which were a feature of the pacifist movement of the thirties. It indicates, among other things, something of the length of time which Donald himself has been on what might be called the road to Aldermaston, the Atomic Weapons Research Establishment in Berkshire, which for a time was the focus, expressed in an annual Eastertide march, of the nuclear disarmaments campaigns of the sixties. Of the five people who went to Tilbury, he is the sole survivor, and the composition of that group represents something of the confusion of motives and attitudes so characteristic of the strongly emotional pacifism of the period. Crozier had been a warrior of note in the war of 1914–18, where his sanguinary methods were sometimes cause of criticism. Subsequently he had, in 1920, commanded the notorious force known as the Auxiliaries who operated with the Black and Tans in Ireland during the troubles of those times. He then resigned, and wrote a book called *Ireland Forever*. His presence, a decade or so later, in the pilgrimage to Tilbury, suggests that he had performed another and even more remarkable *volte-face*.

Maude Royden was an ardent feminist, a great sponsor and representative of women in the ministry, assistant preacher at the City Temple, and the founder, with the Anglican Percy Dearmer, of a church, whose services were for a time an attraction in their day. Donald first encountered her at Cambridge, when she was addressing a meeting. 'I heard the most powerful oratory that I've ever heard in my life. It was tremendous. I got to know her later on the Peace Pledge Union. She was a woman of great intellectual ability, of great drive and character, and fiercely feminine. I can remember on one occasion incautiously saying at one meeting that there were too many women there. She said, "You mean there are too few men".' She died in 1956, all passion spent.

Of Dick Sheppard of St Martin-in-the-Fields we have heard already. Herbert Gray was a Presbyterian minister of much distinction, a writer and a luminary of the Student Christian Movement in its heyday. And Donald then, though in years the junior of the five, was in terms of pacifist conviction the same then as he has remained since—an uncompromising opponent of war and indeed of violence in any form at any time, and in any cause. And then again the composition of this group on its way, as it hoped, to Chopei, was illustrative also of some of the continuing features of pacifism, then and since. There was its power to bring together in common action sharply disparate elements. It would be difficult indeed to find any personalities quite so disparate as General Crozier and Maude Royden. In a much later age, Bertrand Russell found it possible to co-operate, at any rate for a time, in the Campaign for Nuclear Disarmament, with Christians of all sorts and conditions, until the virtual break-up, due to internal pressures, of that body, illustrated yet another characteristic of pacifism—the tendency of those practising it to separate into schismatic groups.

And then again that group on its way to Tilbury seemed to illustrate yet another characteristic of the pacifist position—a belief in the moral approach. This has often been combined not only with a belief in the power of example; but especially, it would seem, a belief in the power of the example of Britain—a belief which may well derive from that country's imperial past, when how Britain acted counted for much, partly because, however unpalatable the fact, she held dominion over palm and pine. The belief of those five people on the way to Tilbury in the early thirties that their action would influence warring Chinese and Japanese obviously contained some of this element, just as the Ban the Bomb movement of later years drew much of its dynamic from the belief that Great Britain, who did not in fact at the time possess the bomb but had borrowed it from the Americans, would render a unique service to mankind by giving it up. And finally, there is evidence here of that strong belief in the power of demonstration which has been a feature of pacifism, and of Donald's pacifism too, all through the years. 'Pacifists thought it possible to preach a sermon to the world which would convert the stony heart of international diplomacy. If that failed then there was always martyrdom, but this martyrdom was still conceived optimistically. One might mount a cross but it was generally in sure and certain hope of resurrection.'[1]

All these, and other elements, heroic, obstinate and immovable, are to be found consistently on Donald's pacifism. Like his Socialism, its basic elements have remained unchanged over the years. But the circumstances in which this pacifism of his has had to be expressed have dramatically altered. The fact that his views have not changed makes of him, by this time, an almost unique figure on the pacifist scene. He survives from one age into another age. He is a living link between pacifism expressed as a personal refusal to take up arms, and a pacifism which can abhor, but can no longer by isolated individual action affect, a situation in which there exists the nuclear equivalent of fifteen tons of TNT for each inhabitant of the globe and in which, therefore, all of us must live

[1] David A. Martin, *Pacifism: An Historical and Sociological Study* (Routledge & Kegan Paul, 1965).

with the possibility of an end of the world with every tick of the clock.

Any account of Donald's pacifism therefore needs to be divided into the two epochs which are now discernible within the whole movement—the age before the Bomb and the period since the advent of that weapon with its Doomsday overtones. It is difficult to pinpoint the time when Donald came out in public as a convinced Christian pacifist. There is no parallel with that moment of truth in the engine sheds at Derby which saw the birth of his Socialism. But pacifism as a general attitude seems to have emerged in him as early as his Cambridge days. He outlined the process briefly in a radio interview. 'Like a great many boys of eleven, when war broke out, I was swept into the psychological environment of the First World War. Almost the first thing I can remember was a pageant at which I sang the Marseillaise, and I very speedily went into uniform. I loved it. I became efficient as a bayonet-fighting instructor. It was only much later, when I went to University, that this whole thing became revolting to me and I began to think in different terms altogether.'

A fuller explanation of this process, which at the same time identifies the kind of pacifism which Donald has practised—and there are many kinds—and places it in historical context, comes from Eric Baker. 'During those years between the wars many Christians became adherents of the Christian pacifist position. This was something that germinated in their minds and then finally found complete expression. But the time when we all date the real beginning of our crusade was in 1935, when the Reverend Henry Carter, a very prominent Methodist minister, published an article in the *Methodist Recorder* which announced his conversion to the pacifist point of view. This immediately resulted in a good many ministers responding to him and suggesting that we should get together. Donald was one of these. That was the beginning of the Methodist Peace Fellowship of which Henry Carter was the founder and the first president. Donald and I were Joint Secretaries until the year after. He remained in the Methodist Peace Fellowship, active in office right the way through, and eventually, after Henry Carter's death, he became the president of it. Those years, 1935–39, were times in which there came finally into being a generation of English youth who might, at any moment, have to make a decision about their personal service, or their refusal of it. The covenant of the Methodist Peace Fellowship, which was accompanied by a service of Holy Communion, was a covenant whereby those taking part covenanted together to have nothing whatever to do with war, to renounce war in all its ways and works as being completely and entirely un-Christian. Donald was one of those who took the first covenant and who renewed it from time to time.

'The rationale of his pacifism is perhaps not very simple. Radically, it is of course that, in his judgement, the Christian religion is a pacifist religion. He cannot square taking part in war with Christian discipleship. But, as with all apprehension which he has of Christian truth, he is quite incapable of holding it in a vacuum, but he always relates it to the whole of the contemporary scene. And so it is inevitable that in his proclamation and exposition of the Christian pacifist position, he always includes other political, related principles which he holds equally with his pacifist principles. That is perhaps what is different in his pacifism from a good many Christian pacifists. Many of them stop at a recognition of the inconsistency of Christianity and war, and do not trouble, as Donald does, to give these same convictions their expression in other fields of political action and propaganda.

The mention of Henry Carter identifies Donald's pacifism as clearly in the tradition of that pacifism which has always been an element within Methodism, as indeed within British nonconformity in general. This strain has a long history, becoming more pronounced as national wars of sovereignty tended to become more and more people's wars. So throughout the nineteenth century nonconformity threw up notable men who expressed unease at the military involvements of their governments. Henry Richard, the Congregationalist, in mid-Victorian times was a pacifist, in so far as the term then existed. The Crimean War saw a division of dissenting opinion; but the Quaker John Bright was clear in opposition to it. The Boer War caused a similar split; but for a time Hugh Price Hughes, the most distinguished Methodist of his day, opposed it. So did Doctor John Clifford, the Baptist. The 1914–18 conflict, the first total war with which the Christian conscience had been faced again caused a split, especially on the issue of conscription and as the length and horror of the war alike increased. Such examples at least demonstrate the truth of Herbert Spencer's dictum that 'unlike the ministers of the Established Church . . . dissenting ministers derived from classes engaged in one or other form of industrial activity, are the least militant of religious functionaries.'

The remark was much truer at the time it was made than it has been subsequently, even it if does indicate the fact that the Established Church, being more closely involved as a majority church with the mainstream of national life, has less freedom to adopt absolutist positions. But such men as Canon Raven, Bishop Barnes of Birmingham, in the years between the wars, Bishop Bell of Chichester in the Second World War, with his protests at the terror tactics of Bomber Command, and Canon Collins of CND in the sixties, have all shown that Herbert Spencer's remark has been long outdated. So has the ardent support given by the Anglican Church to the League of Nations in the years between the wars, and the agonised debates upon the issue of the Church and War at the Lambeth Conferences of 1930 and since. So has the existence of the Anglican Peace Fellowship. The case of Dick Sheppard with his peace Pledge Union, with which Donald was for a long time so closely involved, stands apart as the sentimental journey of an individual.

After the First World War, Free Churchmen, pacifist and non-pacifist, like most other Christians in the Western democracies, set their hopes upon the League of Nations. The Methodist Conference passed numerous resolutions in favour of collective security and disarmament—those strangely self-contradictory terms. The age threw up such bodies as the Fellowship of Reconciliation and the World Alliance for Promoting International Friendship Through the Churches.

Meanwhile, two events had taken place in the early thirties which gave to the pacifist debate a new urgency and new stridency. The first was the emergence, like a manifestation of delayed-action shock, of the literature of the 1914–18 war. Starting with R. C. Sherriff's play, *Journey's End* in 1929, a whole procession of books began to appear. There was Vera Brittain's *Testament of Youth*, Remarque's *All Quiet on the Western Front*, Aldington's *Death of a Hero*, Graves's *Goodbye to All That*, Sassoon's *Memoirs of a Foxhunting Man*, Edmund Blunden's *Undertones of War*. Now at last the truth about the mud and blood and cruelty and ineptitude of those terrible years began to emerge. The impact of these revelations was very great. It was as if the very names on the war memorials began to cry out, and those who heard them were deeply troubled.

The second event which gave not only a new stridency, but also a new urgency, to the pacifist debate of the thirties was the rise of Continental regimes which were frankly militarist in nature and intention. And, in so far as they stressed the need to redress wrongs resulting from the years 1914–18, they were ancestral voices prophesying war. The appalling prospect of a second round therefore opened up. The impossible looked like becoming possible: the unthinkable looked like happening again. The deep perturbation this caused was reflected in many areas of the life of the period. The contortions of the intelligentsia and of the politicians were extraordinary. The dilemma of the churches, caught between the choice of resisting the evils of these new regimes or of giving way to them, was severe indeed. The Methodist church in a declaration on 'The Church and Peace' adopted at its Conference in 1936, recognised that both pacifism and non-pacifism were possible to the Christian conscience. The Baptist Union Council and the Congregational Union were alike uncertain. So, for that matter, seemed everyone else, including the larger Christian bodies. It was in these circumstances that Dick Sheppard launched the Peace Pledge Union and that Donald became involved in it with him. The nature of Donald's pacifism was already clear. He was a Christian pacifist in the tradition of Henry Carter, whose mantle to some extent he took, and of others like him among his predecessors. As with his Socialism, Donald's pacifism has always been an integral part of his religion. Indeed, there have been those who have suggested that the two represent the sum total of it. But the evidence of his labours in such causes as the Order of Christian Witness and the Methodist Sacramental Fellowship refute this utterly, for anyone who cares to look into the matter. The fact is that Donald Soper the Socialist and Pacifist has been on stage so long that the quieter role of Donald Soper the Christian has been overlooked. There is little news, after all, in sincerity and devotion.

But there was a lot of news, from its very beginning, in the Peace Pledge Union. This enterprise of Sheppard's, catching the mood and the need of the time to an astonishing degree, released in many people generous and intense emotion. How Donald himself became involved with it he has himself told.

'I remember very distinctly that I had had some contact with Dick Sheppard. He had given me my first broadcast. Then, one day, he invited me down to see him at Canterbury where he was Dean. I remember being immediately entranced with him. He was a most unusual and attractive character. And I offered myself as a recruit to his Peace Army. There was Brigadier-General Crozier, there was Maude Royden, there was Herbert Gray, and I think I was next in order of seniority. We were pretty strong in the higher order of brass, but we were not very numerous with regard to foot soldiers. Dick, of course, was periodically ill, and then before the war he died. In one sense I'm glad he did. I think the war would have broken his heart. He was an inspirational leader. We took the attitude that if we could—and this was Sheppard's point—have mobilised enough people we could have created a démarche in which a new kind of political ideology could have begun to emerge. In other words, rather like CND, we failed because, quite simply, we hadn't enough personnel to create a political démarche. I think it is numbers that counted when you were considering, for instance, the availability of armies to operate what the politicians wanted. We had a number of great successes in the early days. Looking back, it's quite clear to me, as it was rammed into my head also over the second venture into this field, CND, that what we needed was more than War We Say No, which was our slogan in the days of the PPU, or than Ban the Bomb, the slogan in the days of CND. We needed a philosophy to go with it; we needed to integrate the whole programme of disarmament and pacifism into the kind of system which alone could make it work. Otherwise it was at best an ideal, and at worst a rather attractive and escapist theme. What system could make it work? Only Socialism. Because it is only Socialism which can integrate the community in such a way that it can act peaceably and justly. It is only Socialism which can transfer the ultimate arbitrament away from violence towards order. In the last analysis—and this is the supreme condemnation of the capitalist system—it depends on violence for its ultimate authority and sanction.'

Here, then, is part of the rationale of Donald's pacifism to which Eric Baker referred. Pacifism based upon emotional abhorrence of war was not enough. But the Peace Pledge Union in its day was, as he put it, even if short of hard political thinking, 'a genuine human outcry against the monumental vice and evil of violence'. Sheppard founded it in 1934 when he invited, according to a pamphlet issued by the Union, 'all those who were willing to pledge themselves to renounce war, to send him their names'. The pledge they were required to sign had a deceptive simplicity, 'I Renounce War and I Will Never Support or Sanction Another'. 'Thousands of men and women', said the pamphlet, 'religious, rational, or broadly humanitarian in conviction, have now set their signatures to this pledge and, moving forward from this negative beginning, have set their energies to its positive fulfilment. Like their decision to make a renunciation of war, their ways of acting for the attainment of peace remain individual; each member must find his own most suitable and effective method of creating a warless order of society.'

This, of course, proved more difficult, and the times were desperately against it. How desperate is reflected in an open letter addressed by Sheppard in the thirties to those whom he called The Men Who Matter, presumably the unhappy politicians of the day. 'Gentleman, you mean well. You are honourable men. To the best of your ability you are doing your duty to your country and to humanity. But because of you a shadow has fallen across the sky, and the world has lost its way in the sombre twilight of suspicion and hatred. Because of you mothers are afraid for their children. Because of you civilization itself is in danger.'

And so it went on. Sheppard died, very sad and alone, before the coming of the Second World War, as Donald has said. But the PPU was still alive in 1942 and a list of its sponsors in that year reads like a roll-call of those who had done much for the pacifist movement in the thirties: Vera Brittain, George Llewellyn Davies, Herbert Gray, Lawrence Housman, Aldous Huxley, J. Middleton Murry, Max Plowman, Arthur Ponsonby, Charles E. Raven, Alfred Salter, Donald Soper, Sybil Thorndike, Wilfred Wellcock, Arthur Wragg and the president, George Lansbury, deceased.

This, then, was one of the chief outlets for Donald's pacifism in that period, and the press-cuttings, as usual, show him in action as a propagandist for the cause. A moving variant to the usual pacifist gathering took place at the Armistice Night meeting at the Central Hall, Westminster, in the November of 1937. There was a vacant chair on the platform, with a wreath on it. This was for Dick Sheppard. Some of the speeches on this occasion look, in hindsight, a little odd. Donald said he felt Europe was on the verge of a pacifist landslide, and Doctor Wilhelm

Solzbacher, a German Roman Catholic, testified to the growth of the peace movement among people of his own religion. By the May of 1938, Hurricane fighters of the RAF were roaring overhead as Donald spoke in Uxbridge at a PPU meeting. By the March of 1939, when the scene was darkening, he was saying that Christian pacifists should be a lighthouse to the rest of the world.

When the darkness did come, he was one of the few who did not compromise in any way with his pacifism, becoming increasingly isolated as more and more who had held to that position in previous years found it impossible any longer to do so. For many the choice was agonising; for some it represented a moral dilemma never satisfactorily resolved. Fenner Brockway, an outstanding pacifist of the 1914–18 war, found himself much less clear in his attitude to this one. Vera Brittain, who maintained her pacifism, was ostracised by old friends. For Donald, the preaching of pacifism throughout the war years in open-air at Tower Hill and on Hyde Park Corner, was an undertaking which would have daunted most men. And what of the Peace Pledge Union? He said, 'It wasn't totally ineffective. In the area of human freedom it was largely the pacifist cause which made the conscientious position possible in the Second World War. Had it not been, I think, for Dick Sheppard and the PPU, I doubt very much whether the tribunals would have been set up in anything like the way in which they were, because my experience, and I spoke at hundreds of them, was that though the procedures were harsh, in ninety-nine cases out of a hundred, the judgements were right.'

This is borne out by the facts. The persecution of conscientious objectors which had often been cruel in the first war, was not repeated in the second. 'In the First World War, three COs out of ten had been imprisoned. In the second, only three out of a hundred went to jail for their principles. Only about four thousand of those who were told they must enter the Army, as combatants or non-combatants, maintained their objection to the length of prosecution or court martial.' The tribunals, for one thing, were differently constituted, and there was no War Office representative. In all, 59,192 people claimed conscientious objection, 3,577 received unconditional exemption. Another 28,720 were registered as objectors on the condition of taking up 'approved work', generally on the land.[1]

Donald's memories of some tribunals show that he himself could be irritating, even if effective. An instance is what happened at a tribunal held in Fulham Town Hall. 'I was asked as the witness whether I had told my friend what Jesus had said about fighting. I said I had. I was then asked if I remembered telling him that soldiers were bidden to be content with their wages. I said I had not done so for the very obvious reason that it was not said by Jesus. It was said by John the Baptist, who also went on to say "and do violence to no man", which I said I thought was excellent advice to any soldier. The applicant got off.'

This period of the Second World War in relation to Donald's pacifism may not be left without some instance of his own basic position in his own words. How was it possible, for example, to live with this pacifism on the one hand, and the knowledge of Hitler's concentration camps on the other? He said: 'It never really bothered me as a basic problem. I've been to Auschwitz—I've seen the whole thing, and I still keep the moral stench of it in my nostrils. But to me the answer to this terrible violence never appeared to be the necessity for more violence. I felt Auschwitz was produced by the war. The persecutions of the Jews were not produced by the war; they were there before it. But the actual enormity of mass genocide was the result of going to save the Jews, if people were going to save them. They did not save them, and this is an argument which I think is perfectly sound: if you employ violence, even under the most terrible conditions, you may in fact increase it. I think the war did.'

[1] Angus Calder, *The People's War* (Cape, 1969).

The argument is plain. War and violence are products of war and violence. At some point the black line of succession must be broken. Whether it ever can be is, of course, another matter. In any event both are totally irreconcilable with Christianity. Such was his position. But now, with the end of the Second World War, Donald's pacifism, with that of many others, was to be carried forward into a totally different epoch—the nuclear age. By the end of 1945, with the war over, Europe shattered and the first atom bombs exploded, Donald can still be found pursuing the argument on these traditionalist lines, as well as looking back sadly to the past. A corporal serving in the British Army of the Rhine had written to the *Methodist Recorder* questioning a letter of Donald's to that paper advocating support of the United Nations. How was it possible for pacifist and non-pacifist to act together in the cause of world peace, when the United Nations Organisation essentially relied upon force? Donald replied: 'The individual Christian, whatever his conviction about participation in warmaking, can only work within the general framework of a world which has but lately emerged from such activity. He must not be surprised to find the elements of a wartime outlook, even in the incipient organisations which have sprung up to outlaw war. His attitude to them should be what we fail to make it in relation to the League of Nations, to support them wholeheartedly in principle, and to seek to enthuse them with Christian strategy.'

A convenient bridge between Donald's pre- and post-nuclear pacifism is provided by a debate between himself and John Middleton Murry, published in the magazine *Picture Post* in August 1950. This was a serious discussion. But the background to it had been faintly ludicrous. It had arisen from a speech of Donald's at a 1950 Methodist Conference in Bradford. In this speech he had said, in effect, that if it came to a choice of taking part in a Third World War or allowing Britain to be overrun by Communist forces, he would choose the latter.

This was the occasion already mentioned when the Press Secretary of the Methodist Church found himself besieged by phone calls, and had to consult Sangster, that year's President, for guidance. The Conference was against Donald. The emotion aroused seems to reflect more than the then current anxieties about Stalin's intentions, with the cold war growing hotter. It seems also to reflect something of the emotion aroused in some of his Methodist colleagues, by Donald himself. They did not like him, certainly not on this occasion, and several speakers arose to point out that his views did not reflect those of Methodism in general. However, Donald himself received some 600 letters from the public. Only ten were critical. But the thunderstorm rumbled on. Sir Malcolm Perks, Senior Circuit Steward of the West London Mission, resigned in protest at his Superintendent Minister's views. A lady who wrote to the *Daily Mail* went even further. 'Switching on to the Home Service, just prior to the 6 p.m. news on 9 August, we were horrified to hear that Children's Hour prayers are to be led by the Reverend Donald Soper. In view of this gentleman's recently expressed conviction that Communism in Britain is preferable to another war, surely the BBC, as a publicly subsidised body, should immediately terminate any contracts which he may have had with them.' But the debate with Middleton Murry was of another order. Nowadays, of course, it would have taken place on television and long ago been lost from the records. But here it is spread across four pages of the admirable and justly lamented *Picture Post*, with illustrations of the protagonists as they strolled round Middleton Murry's farm near Diss, in Norfolk.

It was an interesting confrontation. Murry was one of those highly articulate intellectuals whose mental contortions in the great debate of the thirties had been among the most extraordinary. He had been a leading pacifist and a member of the Peace Pledge Union. He had changed his views, however, after the concentration camp revelations. One of his books had been *The Necessity of Pacifism*. Another had been *The Necessity of Communism*. Now, in this discussion with Donald twenty-eight years after the publication of that book, he was saying that unless Communism was resisted by force, there would be no place left with ideological and spiritual freedom to which anyone could escape. The argument concluded with an exchange important for what it has to say of Donald's position at the time.

'You don't know what would happen if one country were to repudiate its capacity to fight, and then make its claim to moral leadership. I'm not suggesting we should submit to Communism by letting ourselves be overrun by it rather than fight it. I merely say, let us buy time, by fighting a new way. Conceivably it may not come off; but it is worth trying. The facts of history afford incontestable evidence that those who take the sword perish by the sword. But we do not know what happens to those who take the sword of the spirit, because we have not tried it out on a large scale. I ask the opportunity of buying time for humanity, if we should ever be faced by these terrible alternatives.'

Yet such arguments had to be continued in a totally different atmosphere after the detonation, by the United States, of the first hydrogen bomb on Eniwetok Atoll on 1 November 1952. A year later the Russians followed suit. The nightmare, still continuing, of living with the possible ending of all things at any moment, had begun. The Eniwetok explosion apparently appalled even those who had created it. A statement of Donald's, in that year designated President of the Conference, reflected the fact. 'Scientists have apparently been surprised and nonplussed by the colossal explosion caused by the hydrogen bomb. I believe we are reaching in this atomic experiment the point of no return. The issue for humanity as a whole is so urgent that proposals from any quarter to ban or abolish atomic and hydrogen bombs should be immediately accepted by every responsible human being. I appeal to Christians everywhere to demand of their governments that whatever the cost and whatever the dangers, such weapons should be entirely outlawed.'

He continued to react sharply to this new horror, and from this time can be found as an anti-Bomb demonstrator before, with the formation of the Campaign for Nuclear Disarmament in 1957, the way was open to the Aldermaston marches with their new techniques of dissent, destined to be applied widely in other fields of protest as the years passed. Thus in April 1954 Donald was seen walking twelve times round Piccadilly Circus in the early evening rush-hour, wearing a cassock and carrying a notice-board which said, Stop The Bomb We Demand World Inspection And Control Of Atomic Energy. The following December he led a petition to Number Ten, Downing Street, accompanied by a dozen men and women carrying petition forms which 500,000 people were alleged to have signed. The deputation included the Labour MPs, Anthony Greenwood, Sydney Silverman, and Anthony Wedgwood Benn. The petition was received in the usual way, together with the letter to the Prime Minister, urging him to take immediate initiative in calling high-level talks with Russia and America. Mr Churchill replied to this.

Dear Doctor Soper,

In a letter of December 31, signed by yourself and others, you express the hope that I would take an immediate initiative in calling high level talks with Russia and America early in the new year, for the purpose of considering anew the problem of reduction and control of armaments.

Her Majesty's Government have in fact invited the governments of the United States, France, the Soviet Union and Canada to hold further meetings of the United Nations Disarmament Sub-Committee on this important matter, in London next month. . . .

Yours faithfully,
Winston S. Churchill

But that was all that did come out of this particular affair. Downing Street should have been full of people for so grave a petition, Donald felt, instead of the twelve, watched by a larger number of the curious. But he persisted. The support which Cyril Garbett, Archbishop of York, gave to the government's decision to manufacture the H Bomb, saddened him because he admired Garbett and respected the wrestling with conscience which clearly had been involved in the decision. 'As a good man', Donald wrote in *Tribune,* 'he revolts against the monstrous evil of nuclear weapons, and indeed against war itself. As a wise man he recognises that the practical aim of any responsible goverment is to create an atmosphere of peace-making as quickly as possible. Yet in the face of the hard facts, he regards the possession of hydrogen bombs by this country as a shield (sic) behind which peace-making may go on. . . . There must be some overwhelmingly potent reason for such an extraordinary conclusion.'

There was such a reason, of course. It was the argument for the deterrent, upon the knife-edge of which we have all lived ever since. Donald never had any time for it. His life-long journey through the years as a pacifist brought him, literally, to the gates of the Atomic Weapons Research Establishment at Aldermaston in 1958, when he was observed walking in heavy rain through the streets of Hounslow on his way thither, at the head of a wet column of men and women and children, while a Dixieland ensemble ahead played 'Alexander's Ragtime Band'. That was in April. In the September of the same year he was back again. This time he was leading some thirty demonstrators, including Doctor Linius Pauling, an American scientist who had been invited over by the CND to speak at Central Hall, Westminster. All sat down outside the wire-mesh main gate. The ritual, in later years to become familiar, then began. Police asked them to move on. They refused. Names were taken, the first one on this occasion being 'Alderman the Reverend Doctor Donald Soper'. The demonstrators then asked to see the director of the establishment, Sir William Penney. They were told he was not there. At 3 p.m. the demonstrators went away. 'It was', Donald said, 'no light-hearted frolic. The march was the beginning and not the end of the intention.'

He was right in both respects. It can be too easily assumed of people whose consciences drive them to public demonstration that they find it easy, or are sufficiently thick-skinned to be unaffected by the derision or distaste they can arouse, or so physically tough as not to mind the man-handlings they sometimes get. None of these things has ever been true of Donald. He was always sensitive; he has for years had physical disabilities which have made any prolonged effort of this sort painful and exhausting; and his abhorrence of violence has not been confined only to the idea of causing it; but also to the possibility of receiving it. These are not the best qualifications for reacting with a good grace to being moved on, or carried off, by the police, or for being regarded as some kind of instant demonstrator driven into the streets by some kind of urge towards exhibitionism. It is true that the engineered, quite often violent, and certainly over-frequent type of demonstration of recent years has debased the currency of protest, and increased the likelihood of counter-protest. But Donald belongs to a generation to whom confrontation with law and order is always a serious matter, and has always to be one of conscience.

Donald's involvement with CND inevitably led him much into this area of public demonstrations. For him, the road to Aldermaston was a natural continuance of his pacifism. But CND itself, as he stresses, has not been necessarily an expression of the pacifist position as such so much as 'the activity of many people who felt that here was a more practical and immediate issue than actual full pacifism—an issue arising out of the enormity of the nuclear threat, which is distinguishable from every other kind of military or naval threat ever known'.

This is not the place to enter into the complex story of the rise and fall of CND, a movement which in its days of maximum impact aroused something of the widespread popular support of the Peace Pledge Union in the thirties, although on a less emotional and more logically considered basis. How it was formed, with Peggy Duff as organising secretary, how it rose to be a major influence on public and political opinion, and how it declined has been lucidly told by Canon John Collins in his book, *Faith Under Fire*.[1] The relevant question here is Donald's involvement, as a life-long pacifist, in the whole thing. And here

[1] John Collins, *Faith Under Fire* (Leslie Frewin, 1966).

it should be said, although the fact is little known, that he was its precursor by virtue of being chairman of a short-lived organisation, the Hydrogen Bomb National Campaign. This arose out of growing anxiety in Britain at the growth of the nuclear arms race, and the announcement by the Government, in April 1954, that Britain intended to develop her own independent deterrent.

Soon, with dramatic developments on the world stage—Suez, the British H-Bomb test on Christmas Island, anxieties about the fall-out effects of the testing generally, and the question of acceptance or rejection of the unilateral disarmament argument as a major issue in the Labour Party, the matter became greatly enlarged. CND was launched, with John Collins as chairman, at a meeting in Central Hall, Westminster, in February 1958. Donald from the first was closely involved. Thereafter he was to be found active in most of the highly organised protest actions in which the campaign specialised.

Of these, that which made the greatest impact on the public mind was the annual Aldermaston March, beginning on Good Friday and ending the following Monday. This demonstration, in the great days of the movement, had many thousands of people involved. Donald led the first of these marches on the second day. Why and for what purpose? He said: 'What is the object of any march of that description? You can think of it in either one of two ways; as a means of changing a policy, or as a means of advocating a change of policy. I think Aldermaston was the second. It was an advocacy. It was a most moving experience. It pelted with rain. We were absolutely soaked. But to see, going through Hayes, the entire Borough Council standing in the rain saluting us as we went by, to see the crowds of people who stood in that drenching rain who really regarded this march as the doorway to a better world, was very moving. But they were wrong, of course, poor creatures. . . . We have always, at home, saved the Saturday after Good Friday as a sort of domestic occasion. This particular Saturday I said to my wife that I thought I ought to go on this march to Aldermaston. She said that she had already made arrangements to go with some other people. Then we had to go and see our eldest daughter and talk to her about it. We found that she was going, too. And that to a certain extent is an example of the way in which, in the very early days of the Aldermaston March, it did make a tremendous appeal to all sorts of people, and gave them a sense of obligation.'

Of the earlier days of CND he said: 'The platform was that this country should unilaterally reject the Bomb, the manufacture and the use of it. But first of all the inference that had to be faced was that we had not got the Bomb. It was part of our alliance with the United States. And therefore, in one sense we could not "Ban the Bomb" unless we repudiated the NATO alliance in which the Bomb was enmeshed. Therefore, in one sense, it was an unrealistic campaign from beginning to end, because we could not repudiate the Bomb, or ban the Bomb, without banning the whole military set-up in which the Bomb was an integrated part.

'Why was I involved if this campaign was unrealistic? Because I wanted the country to ban the Bomb. I saw the programme quite clearly in my own mind. For me the kingdom had come when the Labour Party had accepted the CND position at its conference at Scarborough in 1960. The following year, Hugh Gaitskell had the decision reversed. Had the Labour Party come to power in 1966 with a programme which included CND then of course we should have had an entirely different situation. Britain would have been the chairman of the Third World Movement.'

Illusion or reality? Who can say? The Bomb remains, hideously proliferated. The Aldermaston marches have declined into pitiful shadows of their once-great impressiveness. The pacifist movement itself seems in disarray, like a fine cause rendered irrelevant by new circumstances which it cannot directly affect in the earlier manner of a personal undertaking to reject war. Yet none of the changes and chances which have affected the issue have in any way altered Donald's basic convictions.

'He repeatedly and consistently makes his position clear on the Christian pacifist issues,' wrote the Reverend David Francis, a colleague of Donald's in the Methodist Peace Fellowship, 'and he has not deviated, even under the pressures of some pacifists today to rest content with other kindred activities, and to relegate personal non-violence as no longer very relevant or even practical. Without being obscurantist, he remains patiently and patently consistent. You may not agree with him; but always you know where he stands.'

# 7
# Any Questions

And go always not only to those who want you; but to those who want you most.

John Wesley, *The Twelve Rules of a Helper*

We must begin with people where they are, and not where we like them to be. They are not where our fathers were.

D.O.S.

'I HAVE a rooted objection', Donald once said on radio, when asked about his outdoor speaking on Tower Hill and elsewhere, 'to wasting my time trying to convert timber. I could stay around in churches all the time talking to benches and pews. Now if people won't come to you, then I think you've got to go to them, and I am prepared to be as much of a showman as I think it compatible and decent in order to get the chance to go to them.'

This he has done for so many years that the practice has developed almost its own body of myth and legend, gathered around the associated names of Donald Soper, Tower Hill and Hyde Park. Thus it is alleged that it has so rarely rained between 12.30 and 2 p.m. on Wednesdays on The Hill that weather has never stopped play in this particular match, where Donald is always batting to a crowd's bowling. Then there is the story of how, long ago, soon after the opening of this incredible innings, he was asked if he was married. He said that he was not; but that he soon would be. When he next appeared the ceremony had taken place, and a silver teapot, filled with the collection taken among the crowd, was passed up as a present. There are stories of him being thrown from the wall, of him climbing back, and being pulled down again.

There have been awed calculations as to the number of questions asked by the crowd on The Hill over a given time. Thus one man, who had attended regularly from 1930, affirmed in 1963 that on his observation about fifty questions were answered each week. He further calculated that more than ten thousand must therefore have been asked over that span of years, and he had noticed that they had touched upon almost anything from religion, philosophy, morality and economics to politics and science. He added, not surprisingly, that he had never known the speaker to be lost for a reply. By this time, nearly a decade later, the estimated ten thousand will no doubt have been correspondingly increased.

These statistics, however, can mislead, as can also the alleged variety of inquiry. In essence, as Donald himself said: 'People only really asked three questions: "Where have I come from? Where am I going? How do I get there?"' They are not, of course, asked in those forms; but they are the realities underlying even the most diverse and often seemingly unrelated inquiries. And much of the art of this kind of Mars Hill confrontation lies in guessing the intention and the need behind the actual question. The fact that the most frequent one, recurring time and again in various forms, has been 'Why does God send pain?' has much to say about the human condition. So, for that matter, is the fact that in Donald's experience, it is the most difficult one to answer.

This sort of exchange between speaker and inquirer is by no means always a one-way affair. A crowd can educate the speaker, as Donald has said more than once. And then there are the tales of times when the batsman has been bowled. One such moment dates from as far back as the days of prohibition in America. To a heckler who was describing the evils of the Eighteenth Amendment Donald said: 'Have you been in America?' 'No.' 'Then don't talk of things you know nothing of.'

Instantly, from another part of the crowd, a long-established atheist opponent asked; 'Have you ever been in heaven?'

Such shafts, given and taken, have been an essential part of this sort of occasion. A joke against the speaker, even one so fatuous as the shouted question, 'Who washed up after the Last Supper?' can undo him, as he stands there, utterly exposed to anything that may be thrown his way.

And of course, there is the legend of how the whole thing began. As stated earlier in this tale, it began in 1926 when Donald was a probationer minister in the South London Mission. He went to Tower Hill in answer to a challenge. What happened when he got there he described in a radio talk forty-three years later. 'I went to this place and there was a meeting going on. To a fellow I said "I think I'll have a go myself. How do you start a meeting?" And he said, "Get up on the wall, they'll come." I got up on the wall and nobody came at all. I said, "What do you do now?" He said, "Well, clap your hands." So I said, "Will you clap yours?" He said he would, so we had three rounds of applause and a crowd gathered. When I said we were going to talk about religion, they dispersed: but one or two were left, particularly a gentleman rather like a prophet, who happened to be a Marxist. But he asked me a question and off I started. I've been doing it every week since.'[1]

But all these tales about Tower Hill are in fact misleading. So, for that matter, is Donald's own remark about going into the open air, as some kind of an alternative to speaking to non-existent people in churches. The tales mislead because they tend to give the impression that the whole thing is some kind of a turn, performed as much for the amusement of the crowd as the act of the escapologist on The Hill who has himself chained up and then frees himself. This is a serious mis-representation of a very remarkable part of Donald's ministry, carried out with high seriousness of purpose, demanding great courage and effort, attended often by physical risk, always by discomfort, and receiving, as the years passed, no thanks, no recognition of the extraordinary achievement which it now is. And his own al-

[1] BBC programme 'Five to Ten' (5.1.69).

lusion to it as an alternative to the pulpit misleads because it is, nothing of the sort. It is, as he himself has put it: 'A pro-ministry or a pre-ministry. It is ridiculous to assume that all the spiritual and ecclesiastical accoutrements can attach to an open-air meeting . . . what happens in the open air is that you provide a shop window for the case you want to present. You break down some of the barriers whereby it is less difficult for those who hear you, if you are convincing and sincere, to take other steps which elsewhere will be offered. But to present the full Gospel in the glare, the humour, and the inconsequence of an open air meeting is impossible.'[1]

Quite often, especially of late, even that has not been a recognisable description of what happens on The Hill or in Hyde Park. Perhaps the barriers are becoming more difficult to break down. Perhaps the gallant speaker is tiring; or so overwhelmed by the consciousness of the political and economic chaos of human society that he feels such concerns should come first in what he has to say. The things of God, it is true, do still manage to break in but those of Caesar predominate. The constant factor is that it is a man of God who is speaking and who by his courage and persistence is bearing witness to the faith that is within him. But the going is getting harder, and the sinister possibility arises that the old tradition of a democratic society which could pride itself on free speech and the give and take of argument is dying out, and being replaced by a preference for shouting down rather than hearing out.

Donald, writing in *Tribune* recently, remarked upon this development. The particular forum he was referring to was Hyde Park. What was the place like, he asked, in the far-off twenties? 'The crowds were almost exclusively British, or European. To see a coloured face was a rarity, Last Sunday, at 3 o'clock, I would guess that between 35 and 40 per cent of the crowd was coloured, and of the six speakers who were operating when I began to speak, five were black. Let us make no mistake about it.

[1] D.O.S., *The Advocacy of the Gospel* (Hodder & Stoughton, 1961).

These coloured speakers are exciting, eloquent, and endowed with more lung-power than many of their white competitors. Speakers' Corner today is a race forum, frequently a race cauldron. There has been a profound change in the personnel and the provenance of the meetings themselves. The great figures of the late twenties were Bonor Thompson, the pawkiest wit I ever enjoyed, who could talk about anything or nothing with consummate skill, and Father Vincent McNab who was obviously a saint and manifestly a master of his theological craft.

'Such personalities are lacking today. But so are the representatives of the main political parties. Occasionally the Liberal Party or the Conservative Party mount a platform and make a foray whereas in the past they had a regular stand. However, their record is better than that of the Labour Party which to all intents and purposes has given up Hyde Park as a bad job.... This brings me to the main difference between Hyde Park forty years ago and today. The argument has declined. In the religious sphere, secularism, expressed in what the critics of religion believe to be scientific terms, is no longer the menace that once it was to the Christian advocate, either of the Right or the Left. This does not mean that religion is validated or that Marx is repudiated at Speakers' Corner. What it indicates is a move away from propositions and a preference for protests. Declamation has taken the place of debate and, most regretful of all, there is a marked tendency at the moment to shout down the opponent, rather than to controvert him. Speakers' Corner is a sign of the times and those times have radically changed over the years. The old certainties of Christian, Communist, Socialist, Fundamentalist, have largely wilted and given place to a sort of petulant indecision.'[1]

Yet, for him, the show goes on: the remorseless effort continues. Men—mostly obscure figures out of the crowd—have given to Donald a touching loyalty and service over the years. Two such men were the Kirby brothers, Jack and David, pen-

[1] *Tribune* (26 March 1971).

sioners, obviously hard-up, living in retirement high over a London street. One of these brothers said: 'My brother and I were born within a minute or two of Tower Hill, so we were there when Donald Soper arrived in the middle of the 1920s. One of the first people to welcome him on The Hill was our father, who was with him until the time he died. Donald Soper always referred to him as "the man who looked after me". My father held his coat for him while he was speaking. Father welcomed him because he felt the truth of every word he spoke, and the good that he was doing. My father looked upon him almost, you might say, as a grandson. And I in turn looked after him. He used to get some that would try to be tough, after the meeting, as he went away, and I used to go along with him, always, and for some unknown reason they called me Soper's bodyguard. Just walking along with him seemed to be enough. Donald always looked upon it as a great joke, in one sense. But he was thankful to me in another because, he being a pacifist, if one of these characters had got tough, he wouldn't have retaliated. But knowing me, he knew I would. I wasn't a pacifist. I was an Old Contemptible. Any of those herbs or idiots who tried to muck up the meeting I used to keep a watchful eye on, and give a tip to, that they might find themselves in a mess themselves.'

How did Donald affect men such as these, really and truly? As to that the second Kirby brother said: 'He used to speak about Socialism and religion, but he always used to finish by talking about the Kindgom of God. He wanted it on earth, of course, and used to end with the phrase that "This is how I see things, and this is what I think is right. The Kingdom of God established on earth." It was a known fact, and I speak from experience, that in the offices, after lunch-times on Wednesdays, there came to be a sort of debating society of what Soper had said. We always called him just that—Soper. I think the value of his speaking was the way people used to talk about him after he'd got down. Little groups used to assemble and say, "That man's worth listening to." This seems to me very worthwhile. To tell you the truth, I think the value of his teaching, or talking, or whatever you like to call it, was of terrific importance, and still is. I wish there were more like him, that's all.'

But if this lifetime of open-air speaking is much more than a performance designed merely to catch the passing attention, and if at the same time it is not a specifically evangelistic activity as commonly understood, what in fact is it? One thing may be said immediately. It is a unique event at this moment of time upon the Christian scene. Nobody has ever done it so continually before. Nobody else shows signs of now doing it at all. It could be, of course, that it has become by now an outdated form of communication. It could also be that it has grown into a compulsion for Donald, something that must be done, twice weekly, until the voice finally cracks and the body fails. But it also has, for him, a clearly recognisable place in outdoor Christian witness and this, in a time when such activity is rare in any cause, is a matter of considerable interest.

Christianity, as Donald has said, was born in the open air. From New Testament times, through the ages, it has been spoken of outdoors. The friars in the Middle Ages preached on street corners. Wesley and Whitfield and many another spoke with no roof over them other than the sky. But Donald's speciality at Tower Hill, and at Hyde Park, is not preaching. It is, on the contrary, a third kind of open-air witness of which the first is the mass ceremony, or ritual demonstration, like an open-air Eucharist or one of those cross-carrying demonstrations of the devout which often appear on the television news on the evening of a Good Friday. The second is the open-air service, which, like marriage, is not a thing to be taken in hand unadvisedly, lightly or wantonly. As Donald has said: 'A congregation singing lustily to the Lord, under a roof, sounds a wailing disaster out of doors. The parson who is not accustomed to open-air speaking performs his office with fervour but also with a certain amount of obvious pain, and the general impact of the non-existent crowd is not to commend the Gospel but in many cases to degrade it in people's eyes.'[1]

The third kind of open-air witness is what Donald has been doing for nearly half a century. Its characteristic is that its setting is secular rather than sacred. It naturally follows that nothing in it is sacred; that no holds are barred, and that the speaker is totally exposed. Furthermore, he cannot choose his subject, or pursue anything for long. Another question, or even group of questions, comes at him rapidly, quite possibly from a part of the audience which is not aware of, or is indifferent to, what has been going on elsewhere in the amorphous mass of the crowd. Nor can the speaker become involved in language or argument. If he does, his audience will tend to drift off. He must also accept any question: try never to lose his cool, and never to look for applause or anything even remotely resembling deference. It is a hard business. To the observer of any of Donald's efforts on Tower Hill, or at Hyde Park, the impression given is that a minority in the crowd seems usually to be hostile, and the majority vaguely curious. A further impression is of the appalling effort the performance must require of the speaker.

And what of the questions? Donald has said that, although he does not know all the answers, he thinks he knows most of the questions, in the sense of knowing what they will be about. The majority, strangely enough, are about the Church. Here is a dark fact worthy of consideration. Most questions are about the Church, not, it seems, so much because many are interested in the Church, but because the majority disapprove of it. Or, it may perhaps be said with greater truth, that the majority disapprove of the usually widely inaccurate view which they have of it. The credibility gap here is truly enormous. To listen to some of Donald's questioners even today is to receive the impression of men who have always assumed, as if it were a natural fact, that the Church is a con. They do not, oddly enough, extend this assumption either to Christianity or to Christ. But the Church—

[1] *The Advocacy of the Gospel.*

often thought of as some kind of lie-factory, presided over by bishops in palaces—is an object of attack. Partly, of course, this is just another aspect of the whipping-boy function of the Church throughout the ages. Nor is all the criticism as crude as this picture of these crowd critics might suggest. Donald has for years contended with men who have sincerely believed that, because the Church preaches not only what it does not practise but what is in fact unproved, truth is served by exposing the falsity. Hence such confused questions as: 'You tell us that Jesus wants us to see mankind as the family of God. What about the slave trade, then? What about Christian millionaires?' 'You tell us that Jesus came to bring good news to the poor and to warn the rich. What about property owned by the Church?' and so on. This picture of the Church is hopelessly out of focus and out-of date. But it is worth wondering how such a picture came into being in the first place so that it is now an accepted piece of folk-lore.

Questions about the bible naturally proliferate; but not so much nowadays as formerly. Mostly they are the obvious ones. How can the bible be the Word of God when it is full of contradictions? How do you know the bible is not a fake? Can you deny that some of the New Testament is anti-Semitic? What about the virgin birth in the light of scientific knowledge? The tone and phraseology smack of the nineteenth-century Mechanics Institute. But this kind of questioning seems on the way out now at Tower Hill and Hyde Park.

Another kind—ranked by Donald as second in frequency of occurrence—seems currently to be on the way in. This is the political question, usually arising from some contemporary event, probably something in that day's news. On a recent Wednesday it was noticeable, for example, that Donald bought a paper on his way to Tower Hill. When he got there, the second question arose from the lead story. The occurrence pinpointed the truth of Donald's remark in his *The Advocacy of the Gospel*, that though it was not essential for an outdoor preacher to have any basic philosophy of life, it was very important that he should have read the newspaper. Some of his meetings nowadays, indeed seem made up entirely of political arguments, with Donald batting as a Socialist against, surprisingly enough, a virtually neo-Fascist opposition, sometimes of a very ugly kind. As he remarked in his *Tribune* article, the old Marxist argument seems to have faded away and with it the type of questioner who represented it: well-read in a narrow field, and convinced equally of the truth of his own gospel and of the falsity of anybody else's. The fact is one among several indications that the best days of this open-air speaking are over.

A third area of questioning, where again change is apparent, is the scientific field. Here the time-lag between truth and actuality was for long enormous. The popular notion of the scientist as one who revealed truth and practised precise methods of proof, compared with the religious obscurantist, probably dates from Darwin and *The Origin of Species*. This in turn led to the equally popular idea, nurtured by H. G. Wells, of the scientist as the saviour of mankind, white-coated, all-knowing. Donald, in 1961, said: 'I share a conviction of a very great open-air preacher of the Roman Church, Father Vincent McNab, who said to me, shortly before he died, that there is nothing so perverse as the general picture modern uneducated man has acquired of the scientific cosmogony and of the general status of the man who is called a scientist. True scientists are the most humble of people: but the sordid, squalid, pseudo-science, which comes to us as a kind of residual legacy of the nineteenth century's pride and arrogance, is a continuing source of embarrassment and difficulty to any preacher of the word.[1] But that status of the scientist has gone with the wind, and the white-coated saviour of yesterday's world is coming, with maybe a little more justice, to be seen as a possible destroyer of tomorrow's.

Open-air speaking clearly has a technique dictated by the peculiar conditions laid upon the practitioner. The distinction, therefore, between Donald Soper as an open-air speaker in this

[1] Ibid.

genre, and Donald Soper as a preacher, is total. As a preacher, indeed, over the years, he has been eloquent, cogent in argument, and quite astonishing in variety and precision of vocabulary. Preaching as an art, in fact, is something which he has always deeply respected and has extensively practised. No man could hold congregations which, at the height of his powers, he was holding and can still hold, without the assiduous cultivation of this gift. Some of his all too few books of collected sermons, such as *All His Grace, Aflame with Faith*, and *It is Hard to Work for God*, give some idea of the quality of his preaching. But it is one thing to read and to admire such a passage as this from a sermon on Hopefulness: 'What is outstanding is the note of hopefulness that is constantly sounded by the One who Himself identified his Messianic role with suffering love. The reader of the New Testament will look in vain for any suggestion of melancholy in the character of our Lord. He will also look in vain for effervescence. What he will find is buoyancy. Jesus lived his life under the Cross, but never under the weather, and when he finally came to that Cross, with its pain and loneliness, his hope held him up.' It is quite another thing to hear this actually as it was spoken, with all the vigour and rich tonality of voice. Fortunately, this is actually possible and Donald Soper must be one of the few preachers of note much of whose preaching is preserved on tape and can still be heard. This is due to the fact that Miss Sheila Townson, Warden of the Katherine Price Hughes Hostel of the West London Mission, and for many years a member of Donald's congregation, recorded so much of his preaching and speaking. The tapes still exist, a labour of love, and it is these that make it possible to hear Donald over the years and which also make it possible to substantiate the view that here is one of the most flexible and striking preachers which the Christian cause has had. Of Donald's preaching, Miss Townson said: 'My first attraction to the services at Kingsway was this young man, as he was then, thirty years ago, preaching in such a manner that each person felt that he was speaking individually to them. It seemed more than a coincidence, and other people have expressed this opinion, that he seemed to speak to their condition. His style and his vocabulary appeal to me very much indeed because I love words, and the wealth of the vocabulary which he uses makes it an aesthetically satisfactory performance as I listen to it, as well as something that has made me very conscious of the fact that one could not listen to this man and do nothing about it.'

But the open-air speaker must be prepared for total discontinuity of argument, ready with staccato answers as question follows question. He must be witty and quick if the laugh is not to turn against himself. Somebody once asked Donald what shape was a soul. He replied: 'Oblong', and passed on. But that sort of thing is not easy, and the duty of the speaker, anyway, is not to ridicule his questioner but to find what is in his heart.

Occasionally there is quite a lot in his heart. Tales have come down of encounters in The Hill between Donald and apparently hostile critics which have made this clear. There was a man, long ago, who was one of the most implacable opponents Donald ever had on The Hill. He was against anything spiritual whatever, his theme being scientific socialism as then understood. And then the time came when Donald heard that he was ill at home. He called upon him and found, on the testimony of the man's wife, that at home he was an entirely different person from the formidable adversary of The Hill. He was also in some financial difficulty and Donald was able to help him. He received a shy letter of thanks. And then again, later, there was a Russian refugee, a man of considerable distinction, who, feeling the burdens of loneliness and poverty, used to come and listen to Donald on The Hill and subsequently sought him out privately, and had much talk with him. And yet again, there was a young man who lost his wife in childbirth. He had been an anonymous member of the crowd on The Hill; but now he also came to Donald to ask him to conduct the funeral. This was the contact which turned out to be rewarding and helpful and memorable to both.

But such tales can give the false impression that there is some kind of happy ending waiting at the end of this long journey along the rough road of open-air speaking on Tower Hill and in Hyde Park. There is nothing of the sort. 'And does the road wind uphill all the way? Yea: to the very end!' The proof lies in taking samples of what actually happens at these meetings nowadays. Here, for instance, is an extract from a recent encounter on The Hill. It should be remembered that the voice is not so much speaking as cracking with tension and effort.

'Do I agree with Enoch Powell? On principle, no. I'm not impressed by his pathetic pleas to be understood. I'm not impressed by his ridiculous assertion which smacks of Sir Oswald Mosley, that in the midst of the community there are these sinister influences, and that they are working against the general community. The whole thing is monstrously untrue. . . .'

*Voice in crowd,* 'Do you agree with what he says that if we go into the Common Market, we'll be swallowed up by Europe?'

'I very much doubt whether he said that. You ought to remember that most of Mr Powell's utterances are preceded by ifs and peradventures and wonders. He wonders about the infamy of infiltration. He wonders about the problems of disaster. He wonders about the rivers of blood. You do, too? Well, cheer up, you needn't. Hang on a bit and I'll give you comfort.' (Interruption) 'Now then, what I am saying is that Mr Powell did not say in ten years this country would be swallowed up by Europe. What he said was . . .' (Interruption) 'Now listen. Don't try to ask two questions at once. Let me just answer this question as best I can. You won't listen? Then there's not much I can do with you, is there? . . .'

Half an hour later, when all kinds of questions had been raised in what seemed a madly discursive discussion, there was a painful scene arising out of a remark from the crowd that Pat Arrowsmith, sometime of CND, had fled from England at the time of the Cuban missile crisis. Donald suddenly seemed to become grim.

'If you want to tell us that Miss Arrowsmith is a coward . . .'

*Voice*, 'I didn't say that.'

'No, you're not going to say that. What you would like is to infer a bit of dirt, rather than bring it out into the open. Don't do it! Don't do it! And if you want to sneer at Miss Pat Arrowsmith . . .'

*Voice*, 'I'm not sneering. I'm saying you go on about the bravery on her part, then why did she run to Ireland? Explain it. You're getting ratty, but it's true! Deny it! Well, come on! You're always talking such a lot, but there's a hell of a silence. . . .'

There was indeed a silence; but it seemed to the observer to be a silence of exhaustion. Then Donald went on:

'My silence at the moment is because I am ashamed of you, and I think most of the crowd is, too. I don't mind you disagreeing with Pat Arrowsmith. I don't mind anybody disagreeing with Pat Arrowsmith. But I do fundamentally object, and I think this crowd does, knowing her record, of sneering at her courage. You quote what you read? You didn't read enough, You're still persisting in this? I think I'll leave you. . . .'

Where does the Gospel come in? Here is an answer to that question from concluding moments of a meeting in Hyde Park. This particular occasion had been filmed for television and the presence of cameras, made the crowd even more difficult than usual. There had been furious arguments and some quite dangerous moments. Then Donald said this: 'Whatever the opinions of me—and I get a strong impression from time to time that they are not entirely complimentary—what I am concerned to say is something about Jesus Christ. I will say it now and then get down. I believe that Jesus Christ represents the highest that you know and I know, and that the world is increasingly coming to recognise that what Jesus said is true. And it is for that reason, I think, that we should recognise it. I will tell you one of the things that Jesus does for me. He gives me a sense of buoyancy. He doesn't make me as miserable as some of you.' (Angry shouts.) 'I shall go on advocating what I believe. I believe the world is worth saving, because the people in this world can respond to the ideals which in their better moments they cherish. That is the Gospel—the good advice comes afterwards—the Gospel comes first. The Gospel is the assertion that this is God's world and therefore can be made a world of peace, a world of justice, and I'll go on saying that.'

But when all the stories are told, the quotations made, the prodigious record established of so many years of this outdoor speaking, the questions remain as to whether it has been worth it and what the end product has been. Both are unanswerable. That Donald's efforts in this field have won him much respect is a fact. Thus Harold Wilson paid this tribute to 'his tireless and patient work on Tower Hill and sometimes in other places, which I think one would honour him for if he had done it for ten years and then found himself too busy. But he must be honoured all the more because he has kept it up for nearly half a century. He would have had every excuse to stop at some point.'

He would indeed. Maybe he should have done. But there are few signs that he will, voluntarily. Meanwhile, the pattern persists. Very recently a Tower Hill Wednesday, a cold and uncomfortable December day, began with a staff meeting in Kingsway at 10 a.m. That over, it was noticeable that Donald became seemingly apprehensive as the morning wore on. At five minutes to twelve he set off for Tower Hill. Along Eastcheap a man who had been standing in a shop doorway joined him. This was one of his supporters who regularly came up from Hastings, where he lived in retirement, to be with him. A little further along another man, equally elderly, joined the two. On The Hill Donald used the paper he had bought in order to scan the headlines, to drape over the speaker's rostrum he used, loaned to him by the Catholic Evidence Guild.

It was a very rough meeting and there were some harsh exchanges. When it was over, and Donald got down from the rostrum, he seemed quite shaky and exhausted. On the way back to Kingsway he asked whether he had given an impression of being too rough with some of his questioners. When he was told that in fact such had been the impression, he said: 'That's just what my father used to say.' Was he nervous at these meetings? He said, 'Yes; I begin to get nervy as the time draws on. After all, you never know who you're going to meet.' Then he asked, 'Did it seem worthwhile?'

That was not for a mere observer to answer. He has, in fact, supplied the answer himself, writing of a meeting he had had one Wednesday in Holy Week on Tower Hill. 'To seize those moments, not asking for any reward, save that of knowing we do his will, to declare one's own faith, to commend one's own Lord, and to say to those who never darken the doors of the church something about the Cross of Christ is sheer and unlimited joy, and is a reward of priceless worth. I can remember how the words of that meeting concluded and I will repeat them to you. I spoke of Jesus upon the Cross. The crowd was silent. One man wanted to interrupt and somebody told him to shut up. He shut up. And I was able to go on, and I finally said, "I believe, my friends, that there is life in a look at the crucified one." That was my reward, and I believe that by God's grace, a not unworthy fulfilment of a piece of my ministry.'

8

# Late Night Line-up

What do I think about the death of God? I hadn't heard he was unwell.

D.O.S. in an airport interview in the U.S.

When I began my ministry, I was trying to hold on to about three hundred and fifty different theological propositions. . . . Now I can say without truculence, and certainly without any kind of impropriety, the truths I know hold me, and I am content to be dubious about many other things.

D.O.S. in *The Advocacy of the Gospel*

I say now that I rest in this confidence; that Jesus is the way, the truth and the life. On those rations—iron rations if you like —I think I shall probably go the rest of my journey.

D.O.S. on BBC Radio

An old lady in my church said to me that she never knew what fellowship was until she went to Bingo. Then I began by laughing; I ended almost by crying, because it is a most penetrating analysis of the emptiness of so much that goes for what is called modern affluent society.

D.O.S. in House of Lords, *Hansard* 11 June 1969

ON SOME days now, provided that Parliament is in session, it is possible to encounter, between the Abbey and Big Ben, a white-haired man in a black cassock. He limps noticeably, owing to an arthritic hip which has been a painful companion, stoically endured, of his journey through the years. This is Lord Soper of Kingsway, Baron and Life Peer, in his late sixties, and he will be either approaching or leaving the House of Lords. The cassock is his costume in that place. What his costume should actually be was in fact the subject of a commission of inquiry on his elevation to the Life Peerage in 1965. There was no precedent. Bishops, of course, there were already. But a Methodist minister presented obvious sartorial difficulties. He could not wear surplice and lawn sleeves. On the other hand, he should be somehow identified. The cassock was held, after due consideration, to offer an ideal compromise. And since it was a garment that Donald had worn habitually for many years, it presented no difficulties. So cassock it was, and has remained.

Life peers have become, of course, rather more of a familiar part of the contemporary scene since then. But a Methodist minister, especially one nominated on the political list, has remained unique. The fact has given Donald, indeed, two esoteric firsts, still unchallenged. He was the first man to appear in a stained-glass window during his lifetime, and the first Methodist minister to enter the Lords.

The stained-glass window, placed, back in the thirties, in the Muswell Hill Methodist Church, may have aroused no criticism. The same could not be said, however, of his acceptance of this life peerage. There was a flurry of disapproval among some who seemed to think that a life-long rebel had sold out to the Establishment. There were also some of the Establishment who expressed a certain unease at such a person being admitted. Among these, Donald's remark that 'If you want the Lords to be useful you must do something to get rid of the effete hereditary peers', did not help, and the *Daily Telegraph* wondered rather acidly whether he would be able to adapt the tactics of Tower Hill to this very different other place. It was left to the *Sunday Telegraph* to pose an interesting question still unchallenged. Did not this appointment, it asked, raise the issue as to whether there was any reason why the Archbishop of Westminster, the General of the Salvation Army, the Moderator of the Church of Scotland, and the Chief Rabbi, should not henceforth also be numbered among the Lords Spiritual?

Donald himself gave three reasons for accepting his peerage. The first was that he felt that, if there were to be religious representation in the House of Lords, it ought not to be left entirely to the Church of England. Secondly, he felt that this position in the Lords would help him in promoting his own ideals, socialism especially, and, thirdly, he felt that the whole thing presented opportunities to him of championing causes which he had long held dear, in addition to political ones. He added at the same time that the Anglican bishops in the Lords had welcomed him with great warmth.

His maiden speech, apart from its brilliance, was typical in two respects: its seriousness was shot through with humour, and it was delivered entirely without notes. The humour came at the beginning: 'I thought it not inappropriate, in speaking for the first time, and as I think probably as the first Methodist minister, so to occupy your Lordships' time in this place, to consult my ecclesiastical father in God, John Wesley, about this House: and so I did. And, trawling through John Wesley's immortal *Journal,* I find that there is only one reference. I approached this problem with a certain diffidence, because I am bound to communicate to your Lordships that John Wesley was a High Tory, but it may be of some comfort to my noble friends that he himself said he was a very bad one. He says on January 25, in his diary of 1785, "I spent two or three hours in the House of Lords. What is a lord but a sinner born to die?"'

In this manner, then, Donald arrived in the Lords. Since then he has been a frequent contributor to debates. *Hansard* shows him as speaking more than sixty times between 1965–70, mostly on social and ethical questions, but often on political matters of moment, such as the rights of minorities in Northern Ireland in 1968, and arms for South Africa in 1970. His style, as *Hansard* reveals it, is interesting. It is as though here is a different Soper altogether from the Donald of the pulpit or the outdoor stand, speaking as one who, in the maturity of his later years, has developed yet another manner, impressive, excellently attuned to time and place, and on occasions very tough. Thus, on the subject of the Reverend Ian Paisley: 'Mr Ian Paisley has been described, first of all much more widely than in the particular areas of Northern Ireland, as a Presbyterian. He is not a Presbyterian. He is what is called a Free Presbyterian, and the adjective there is quite as inaccurate as the noun. He is not a Protestant leader, as one incautious statement averred only a few days ago. He is certainly not a Protestant in the accepted and traditional sense in which I claim to be a member of that great tradition. He is very largely the author of the particular church which he has spawned. . . . He is a man of bony appearance and of a loud voice. . . . I assure this House that Mr Ian Paisley has been immensely overpraised for qualities which he does not possess. He is a rabble rouser.'[1]

At other times he can be equally intense. Thus in the debate on the Defence Estimate in 1968: 'If we are considering nuclear war, I would respectfully suggest to your Lordships that we are talking in an asylum rather than in any respectable and reasonable place. The sheer concept of what nuclear war means is beclouded by words like "second-strike retaliatory action", "massive riposte", or "conditioned riposte". Sooner or later we become conditioned by these words, and fail to see that the only option we have is to prevent a nuclear war starting: because, if it did start, there would be no calculable end to it, except as I see it, a large-scale destruction of life as we know it. . . .'

James Cameron, the journalist, writing of Donald's life peerage at the time of its conferring, remarked that Mr Wilson had made peers out of two of the most honourable Englishmen alive, Fenner Brockway and Donald Soper. It was not a comment with which all would agree. But it was an opinion well worth having from so seasoned and sagacious an observer, upon an honour which came to Donald at a good time, when most of his years were behind him but while he had yet much to give.

But he is old enough now for it to be possible to try and assess something of what he has been, what he has achieved, what he has become. The white-haired man in the black cassock, limping round Parliament Square these days is a world away—in fact

[1] *Hansard* (3.12.68).

several worlds away, because so much has happened meanwhile—from the rumbustious probationary minister, bursting with energy, who came down from Cambridge to the Old Kent Road nearly half a century ago. Three questions were asked, and answered, about that younger Donald Soper earlier in this narrative. What kind of a man, judging by his impact on others, was he? What was he thinking of the way things were going with the world? What was the essence of the message he felt himself bound to proclaim? If those questions are up-dated now in the seventies, some very interesting answers result. They are also important answers in that they show how dramatically the human scene in general, and in particular the Christian scene, has changed over the years. And they are valuable answers because Donald has always been a man of the moment, reacting instantly to the events of the hour.

He has, inevitably, paid the penalty for this propensity to the instant opinion. Any communicator, in so fast-moving a world as today's, must risk being judged ephemeral by the slower witted. The idea that a man can be both a quick and a profound thinker is not yet generally accepted. It is only when the quick thinking which led to the instant comment of twenty or thirty years ago turns out to be today's truth that the depth of the thought becomes apparent. Thus Donald was saying decades ago that the institutional Church was in decline, and was violently contradicted. The Methodist Conference of 1958, for instance, saw him involved in considerable dispute on this point. But now the truth of the statement is apparent, and the present Secretary of the Methodist Conference, Kenneth Greet, acknowledged the fact in an article in the *Christian Citizen* in 1971, at the same time sensibly observing that the decline applied to all churches, but that some were more aware of it than others. Again, Donald has been quoting for a lifetime an even older prediction that they that take the sword are likely to perish by so doing. Given the present proliferation of nuclear weapons, that has now become at least a probability.

Similarly, any man who lives among today's news inevitably suffers from the fact that there is nothing deader than yesterday's newspaper, and that his views, as expressed therein, are likely to seem so in tomorrow's. Thus some of Donald's comments, when sifted through in the files, tend to have the rustle of dead leaves. He has said something about nearly everything: hunting is sin; the sentences on the Great Train Robbers were un-Christian; sex without marriage is dangerous; life in space is possible; public attitudes to the Profumo affair showed decadence; euthanasia, in certain conditions of incurable pain, was permissible; Apartheid should be boycotted, and so on. But there is a consistency here. In and out of all these issues there runs the thread of the same Christian, Socialist, pacifist, and humanitarian conviction. It would have been easier, of course, to keep silent. But that would have meant the absence, over so many years, of a Christian voice speaking about things on which Christians ought surely to have something to say, and in places where they should surely be heard, and not tomorrow, or yesterday, but now, as the presses roll and the news bulletins go out.

But what are the answers to those three questions about Donald? What kind of a man, judging by his impact on others, has this extraordinary individual become by now? That is not an easy one to answer. Perhaps he is still essentially a solitary, alone in himself although living publicly, still indefatigably on his rostrum addressing the passing crowds in Vanity Fair. He has continued to irritate people, including some members of his own Church, in spite of their admiration for this burning and shining light. Derrick Greeves, sometime minister of the Central Hall, Westminster, though far from sharing such disapproval, had this to say in explanation: 'Increasingly there has been a sector of Methodism that has been staunchly Tory, so that Donald's left-wing views have come under suspicion. And I think the plain truth is that there is a certain type of person who will not accept anything from somebody who is in a different political camp. Then I think it is true to say that Donald has been ahead of his denomination. I think we have now come to accept certain liturgical practices and habits of ecclesiastical dress which have long been, to Donald, just a natural part of taking worship seriously. But his wearing of a cassock and his emphasis on the Eucharist as the central act of worship of the church—these would, to many, in the early days of his ministry, be like a red rag to a bull. I think the opposition has often been focused in those who were staunch evangelicals—he has said some fairly rough things to the Protestant underworld, as he calls this, and has made no bones about it that he is opposed to the average mass-evangelist.

'This does not mean that he wipes them off the map as being useless. But they run contrary to his own intellectual and sociological approach, and they are in a different category of thought to his own. And of course, he has been so emphatically liberal in theology, and ready to admit agnosticism, that some of his ministerial brethren, let alone evangelical laymen, have been critical of him. Another factor is that he has increasingly become *the* Methodist in the eyes of the man in the street, and people who have not the courage to be out in the front representing their denomination themselves, are terribly sensitive about anybody who speaks for them, and who may tarnish what they think is their own image. So Donald is unjustly criticised, I think, by very many because he gets quoted in the Press and on the radio, and this for some, especially if he speaks on a pacifist issue, is liable to be offensive. But attacks have never made him bitter, and this is the stature of the man.'

On the other hand, he has continued to arouse admiration, often from persons not easily given to praise. Thus Michael Foot: 'He has a marvellous charm. Whenever you meet him, and I've met him sometimes in hospitals and other places when he's been ill, you go in and within a few seconds you find that his company is extremely exhilarating. He has a natural charm which has enabled him to overcome a whole host of problems. Then I think he has an extremely clear brain, and a determination to translate his religious ideas into terms of social change. He has, too, great courage, because he has stood out against apparently popular movements in the Church and elsewhere at great cost to himself. Nobody could possibly underrate his courage, particularly in view of the physical hardships that he has had to overcome.'

But the real essence of the man, the real Donald Soper, will probably always be a hidden thing, maybe even from himself. The second question, as to what he thinks of the prospect before that world which he has so busily observed for so long, can be clearly answered. Writing recently, in *Kingsway*, the magazine of the West London Mission, he said: 'There seems to be a growing conviction, among those who are thought to be experts in descrying the signs of the times, that we are moving into one of the larger crises of our human affairs. Are we at the end of an era of traditional capitalism? Quite apart from the question as to whether it is a good or bad, is it not rapidly becoming unworkable, and have not the conditions of the modern technological and scientific society, plus the increasing tensions which they bring with them, rendered this system inoperable . . .? A bigger question still is whether our Christian morality is strong enough to sustain the shocks of the modern world. I believe . . . that we are at the end of an age.' But he added: 'I believe that the Gospel still is the good news for a world at the end of its tether. In fact I believe that only those who see the present situation as the end of an age are likely to look to Christianity as the necessary beginning of a new and better one.'

Such a view is a long way indeed from the confidence of one who preached of the Kingdom of God on earth as an attainable possibility through social and political action. Or is it in fact a view more consonant with that element in the New Testament which, adapting and adopting some of the apocalyptic teachings of parts of the Old, speaks of a new age as possible only after many things of this world have passed away?

The answer to the third question, as to the nature of the message he feels it his duty to proclaim, is much more difficult to get at, if only because the Donald Soper of today seems to be more concerned with the importance of living his faith, than with that of talking about it. As he has said, the number of doctrinal positions he now finds it possible either to hold or think necessary to define is much less than it once was. 'I would think,' he said in a radio interview, 'that to maintain a belief in Christianity in any set form of words becomes increasingly outmoded unless those words are capable of a considerable elasticity. And as I grow older—old if you like—I do not find it imperative any longer to collate all these various propositions, and to say this is, so to speak, the substance of my faith. I believe in Jesus, and I believe in him as Lord, and to say Jesus is Lord and to say he is the way and the truth and the life seems to me far more satisfying than to be able to recite a series of catechisms which, nevertheless, are true.'[1]

This scaling down of definite doctrinal positions he is prepared to hold has been accompanied by marked changes in his views on the institutional Church and its future. He has sometimes expressed these views with considerable violence. 'I have to confess that I do not believe in the Church any longer. . . . The Church is no longer a viable institution for the expression of Christianity and for the good of the world.' Both of these statements came in a television interview, suitably enough called 'At the Eleventh Hour', not long ago. But each does less than justice to the reality and depth of his thought and belief in this area. This can far better be found in the relaxed atmosphere of private discussions.

So what does he really think about the future of the institutional Church? Certainly he believes that it will have to be radically and fundamentally different from its present form, and that its need for change is so great and so pressing as to pass far beyond what could ever be achieved by any adaptation of present structures. Here again he has made, from time to time, fairly wild statements, but those who take note of them ought to remember that Donald has always been an almost dedicated controversialist.

[1] *The Time of my Life* (5.1.69).

Thus it is not so long ago since he wrote that he would bar all reading of the Bible for a trial period of one year, and that he would decree, if he could, that every other sermon preached in a public place should take a political text, and should expound that text in relationship to the government of the day and in the light of the teaching of Christ.

But privately he is much more restrained. What does he really feel then, concerning the future of the institutional Church? He said that he felt certain that there would be great changes intellectually within it, and that these were so necessary that the institutional Church of tomorrow—or the day after tomorrow—would have to be radically and fundamentally different in many of its aspects from the Church of today. For one, he did not think it possible that any church in time to come could possibly be geared to Sunday, and that, since Sabbatarianism had never been any use to Christianity, this would be no loss. Tomorrow's Christianity would, on the contrary, 'define its milieu in a seven-day week'. Worship would come to be seen as a natural activity of a weekday, in the midst of the working world, and combined with this would be a recognition of the value of some church buildings as holy places set apart, to which the wayfaring man could retire for a while before going back into the world.

Even more fundamental, in his view, would be the need for the Church to live on a different intellectual diet in times to come. He could not resist, even in this area, a characteristic facetiousness. 'Many now have indigestion: others more serious stomachic conditions, and some permanent ulcers.' In any event, it was no longer possible to frame anything like a theological statement about ultimate reality in the precise way in which scientific and technological inquiry has found it necessary for its own purposes of definition. What then of the creeds? He said that he was prepared to stand before them, as it were as a seigneur in the days of chivalry stood before the heraldic emblems of his forefathers, and would repeat these creeds in honour of his forebears in the faith and in recognition of the continuity of belief. He added that the business of the Church will not be so geared as now to proclamation of indisputable or impeccable statements which the faithful are required to accept. The day for such dogmatism is over.

And then again, in his view, the institutional Church will have to accommodate itself to new and much more practical relations with government. Increasingly, responsibilities of government will extend into areas which were once the monopoly of the Church. Even now, he added, government is recognising that if it really wants to further the cause of social reform it requires the assistance of voluntary bodies and that the Church is a very important element among them. Does this not then argue the emergence of what is wholly a servant Church? His answer here was that if a man believes, as a Christian is entitled to believe, if not in the perfectability of man, then at least in his capacity to achieve a just social order, then his Church cannot rest content to be a remnant Church: it must be a servant Church. A remnant Church is a negative Church. It recognises that ultimate objectives cannot be achieved in this world and is therefore concerned to preserve those seeds of good which can only gestate in another, wherever and whatever that may be. But a servant Church is committed to the belief that the ideals for which Christianity stands are attainable, and must be striven after. But in performing this service for society, the Church should not regard itself as either unique or exclusive; but as a body which acts out of love. Its services to society will therefore be rendered with that motive alone, untouched by any desire for self-aggrandisement.

What, then, is to happen to the proclamatory function of the Church? Here he felt that the idea of preaching as enunciating a plan of salvation, unique and mysterious, is disappearing and should disappear. Preaching 'has to be the communication of ways of service rather than of supernatural ways of grace. This does not mean that the means of grace are not supernatural. What it does mean is that preaching must be concentrated on the Kingdom of God of which we are servants, rather than upon the supernatural Kindgom of Heaven of which we are heirs.'

But, if this be so, at what point is the Church of tomorrow to teach the facts of the faith? In other words, in this new shape of the Church, how are the historical facts of the faith to be transmitted? He said: 'The Bible is an indispensable instrument here. And those of us who take radical views of it must not neglect its source value. We have to teach what Jesus said and did—the historic events of the faith. Christianity is an historical religion, otherwise it is good advice; not good news.'

What did he mean, then, when, writing in *Kingsway*, the magazine of the West London Mission, he said that Christianity was 'in a terminal condition'? He said, 'We have for long enough tried to patch up elements in Christian ideology by ecclesiasticism. This must now be allowed to die, because it has no real vitality. In this sense, we have come to the end of an age.' He added that we have also come to the end of a long era when sedentariness and separateness were imposed on most people by difficulties of communication. Now there is possible a new immediacy, a new knowledge of what is happening in global terms. It followed that we can no longer honestly think in terms of separate and isolated institutions. One consequence of this was that in religion we were at the end of an age in which Christianity could be regarded as the exclusive religion, with a monopoly of the truth, and when others could be regarded, as it were, in the darkness of primordial night.

Again, he felt that we have reached the end of an age of physical incompetence when we could not change human nature. Now there is a possibility already looming over the genetic horizon, to take one field alone, of man-induced changing of personality, of selection of sex, of a whole host of possibilities where, for the first time, man could by his own hand manipulate human nature at its point of origin. Here, as elsewhere, the so-called 'acts of God' were going to be reduced to a very small compass indeed. We were now seeing in the psychological field what happened in the physical field in the nineteenth century, when God was driven out of the physical cracks of the universe. He was now being driven out of the psychological cracks as well.

But he did not mean the end of the faith when he said that Christianity was in a terminal condition. He had meant the end of an epoch in that faith.

What, then, were the 'iron rations' of the faith which he himself now lived by? He said: 'I am not sure that I live by a faith today as live by a kind of dynamism or activity, a drive. I find satisfaction in activity, in the prosecution of ideas, although these ideas would elude my comprehension if I tried to write them down in too precise a form. This is another way of saying that a basic element in my Christian faith is obedience to things which I believe to be true which require the illustration and the dynamic example of someone who lights them up. It is in this regard that my allegiance to Jesus comes in second. I hear him speak, and I am gripped by the word, and having embraced the word, I have to go back to him. What comes first is the act of confidence in the worthwhileness of optimism, of love, of peace. By an effort of will I have to get free of the framework of cynicism and suspicion. I do not believe that, except in the ultimate sense, God takes the first step. I believe I do. I have never subscribed to the idea of the helplessness of man. There is an element of choice which man has to make, however small it is. I make one faltering step. God comes the rest of the way. But I have to make that first step and, for me, it has to be a world-embracing attitude.'

It is an interesting credo, the statement of a man concerned beyond all else to be honest. But that it is also the credo of a man as deeply concerned with, and committed to, truth as revealed in Christ Jesus, no one who takes a long and hard look at the work and witness of Donald Soper over the years can possibly doubt. If he has had a weakness, it is a preference for those very things to which he refers in his statement—dynamism and action. It may be that this has at times retarded the development of a depth of spirituality of which, given other compulsions, he may well have been capable. But in this, as in so much else, he is a man of his times. '"In our time the road to holiness passes through the world of action" wrote Dag Hammerskjold, and it is quoted approvingly by religious writers. But our problem is not that we take refuge from action in spiritual things; but that we take refuge from spiritual things in action.'[1]

It is too early to say whether this has in some measure happened to Donald Soper. Meanwhile, the extraordinary achievement of his rich, infinitely varied and always courageous ministry stands. It is now thirty-six years since he went to the West London Mission and he is there still. It is true that, in common with many other similar places, the days of the great congregation are over. But the work goes on and the social witness is as strong and variegated and vigorous as ever. And still, every Wednesday, the same man climbs his rostrum on Tower Hill at 12.30 and speaks over the crowd in his gravelly voice. Still on Sundays he is to be found in Hyde Park. Still, wherever he feels there is a wrong to be righted or a cause, especially a minority cause, to be furthered, he is there, at whatever the cost in physical or nervous effort. If he has been the great demonstrator, the continual odd man out, it has been done at a price, and that price has been high. Thus it follows that one of the most outstanding features of his life and witness has been courage. And when the time comes, as it comes for all men, for that life to close, it will be possible to think, in relation to it, of those passing words of Christian in *Pilgrim's Progress*: 'My sword I give to him that shall succeed me in my pilgrimage, and my courage and skill to him that can get it.'

He was asked once, typically enough in a radio interview, as to whether he ever thought of his own death and, if he did, whether it frightened him. He replied: 'It doesn't exactly frighten me. It saddens me. I wish it weren't going to happen. I don't like getting old; I don't enjoy it. But I would take my comfort from believing that God is my father and I must put myself in his hands, and that which is self-conscious in this world, that which is I

[1] Monica Furlong, *Travelling In* (Hodder & Stoughton, 1971).

in this world, is imperishable, and therefore, to be with God is everything.'

But the last word ought to be with a distinguished member of his own church, Harold Roberts. 'He has been able, in ways that others have not succeeded in achieving, to establish contacts with the outsider. I do not suppose that there is any minister—certainly not in our church—who has such substantial contact with people who are outside the churches. And if I were asked, if he were to begin his ministry today, whether it would be an advantage if he took a different pattern I would say "Certainly not". He might wish to adapt it in certain ways. But I'm pretty sure that the pattern of his ministry would be much the same. The heart of it is caring: caring for God and caring for people. And I think that in so doing he has been following out the summing up of the Gospel by Jesus himself: "Thou shalt care for the Lord thy God, and thou shalt care for thy neighbour as thyself". I know of nobody who has succeeded in doing that so clearly, so potently, in our ministry, as Donald Soper.'

# Epilogue

IT COULD have been any other morning, of any of the other many years of his life, upon which Donald Soper had gone down from his home in Hampstead to his office in the West London Mission above the Kingsway Hall. But it wasn't. Although he looked much the same as ever, wore the same cassock, sat in the same worn chair, there seemed about the place an unmistakable air of an ending. It was an accurate impression. Within a week it was to close down, and though the work was to continue elsewhere with vigour, the building which for well over forty years had meant so much to Donald was to pass to other hands for other uses.

It would have been unnatural if he had not felt regrets. He was to have a room, he explained, elsewhere where daily he could go, and would, after the pattern of a lifetime, whenever, that is, he was not posting to and fro, again after the pattern of a lifetime, upon any of his many commitments. Most of them seemed to involve the media. That very week he had been on either radio or television three times. All occasions had involved issues of the day, from abortion to various political questions. He was due, also, shortly to fly out to San Diego, California, there to debate with the Creationists who had sprung up in those and other parts in recent times to challenge long accepted Darwinian theories and to replace them by Bible based doctrines of creation.

This return to Genesis struck Donald as peculiar, interesting, and mistaken. He intended, he said, to smite them hip and thigh, and was looking forward to it keenly.

Here was the old adversarial situation still in action. Here was yet another bull for this tireless matador to take on. Here in fact, to change the metaphor, was the man in the headlines still in action, a first choice of many a current affairs producer for instant comment and ready debate. In Broadcasting House, in Television Centre, in the studios of Independent Television, his name was still sure to be on file near the phone. He had, he said, on that spring morning in Kingsway Hall, 'been having a rough time lately', meaning that those phones had been ringing and that he had been answering the summons to speak, to appear, to argue. Two recent adversaries had been Mr St John Stevas and the Bishop of London: two recent issues the Pope's views on some moral questions, which Donald held to be dangerously reactionary, and some remarks of the Archbishop of Canterbury, which Donald had felt to be unnecessarily war-like. Clearly, he had been greatly enjoying this rough time. His body, he remarked, might be showing signs of wear and tear; but his mind felt as clear as ever, except for the fact that he was no longer able to remember musical tunes with the same facility as in former times. But when the adrenalin was running he experienced no diminution of powers whatever.

He was seventy nine. The question must arise as to why a man of such an age should continue to be so much in demand for that particular kind of activity. The answer is plain: he has had few, if any, successors as a Christian spokesman highly skilled in the kind of quick thinking demanded by the role of instant commentator. The origins of this skill, and of the constant practise in it, had obviously derived from Tower Hill and Speakers Corner in Hyde Park. And though the knockabout nature of those encounters with the crowd changes to a far more civilised form of confrontation within the disciplines of the studio, the essence of the matter is still instant Christian comment within the context of current events. The crowd is still present, and a very large one. Invisible behind a microphone and camera, sitting at home rather than standing under the sky, it is just as critical, and at times just as unforgiving. Why then has he had so few successors? It is a fact which he keenly regrets. He said: 'I wish some parsons had come along to try this kind of thing. But they don't seem to'. He will not say so himself; but the possibility exists that few indeed are able. Many may be called; few appear, even if chosen, to have what it takes to measure up to this very severe form of challenge with the unique expertise which has been his for so long.

There may, of course, be deeper reasons why he seems to have had no successors, so that the producer in need of quick Christian comment still goes on dialling the Soper number.

The principles which moved Donald to speak outdoors still stand — that it is necessary to go out to people rather than waiting for them to come to you. It is still true that Christianity was first preached in the open air, and has continued to be so in various forms and places. The friars did it in the Middle Ages; the Salvation Army began by doing it and have continued; the TV Churches of recent years in the United States do it now on a vast scale, even though their doctrines appear to some to be dangerously misleading. The words of John Wesley are still relevant: 'and go always not to those who want you; but to those who want you most'. Donald's own words are still relevant, too: 'we must begin with people where they are, and not where we would like them to be'. Yet the main stream churches, so called, seem to have withdrawn from this kind of dialogue. An even deeper reason why this is so could be, of course, that they have lost confidence to some extent to what they have to say. Or again it could be that what they have to say has become too complex for simple statements. Whatever the reasons the loss is a sad one, and when Soper's voice at last falls silent it is difficult indeed to see whose will take its place. Meanwhile he carries on; the going has become harder. The outdoor form has become increasingly the area of bitter racist issues; the level of debate has continued to decline, and invective to take the place of arguments.

Donald retired from the superintendency of the West London Mission in 1978. The fact that he was still using a room there represented an arrangement of grace and favour rather than a position of authority. His retirement ceremony, if it could be so called, was an interesting occasion. The great hall at Kingsway was packed. All sorts of conditions seemed to be present, and all ages.

The chain of office of the Mayor of a London borough gleamed upon the platform. The white hair of Michael Foot was prominent. It was he who said, in one of the several addresses, that when, years before, his mother had suspected that his Christian conviction did not seem all that it should have been she sent him to Donald Soper. The result, Foot said, was that if he did not learn a great deal more about Christianity, he certainly learnt a lot about politics.

But two features of this retirement occasion gave a rather different impression. The first was a remark made, by another platform speaker, that he knew of many people in that gathering whose lives had been touched for good, who have been helped in all kinds of ways, and of others who, when they have been lame dogs, had been assisted over all manner of stiles by Donald Soper.

The other feature was of a very different nature. It was an altar, placed prominently if incongruously in the centre of the platform, and obviously a fixture. With its frontal, its cross and candlesticks, it was something which could scarcely have been found in that position in 1936 when Donald had followed the famous Hugh Price Hughes into the superintendency of the Mission. What it represented had been central to Donald's ministry always. 'The sacrament of the Lord's Supper provides the authentic and actual means whereby decisions can be expressed and discipleship begun in the Christian life', he had written long ago in the Bulletin of that Methodist Sacramental Fellowship with which he had long been associated and of which he became President in 1950. This in its time had been a movement against the tide of much traditional Methodism. But he had always insisted that he was but following the usage of the Wesley's themselves.

So there this altar stood, on the platform in Kingsway Hall, on the afternoon of his retirement, an outward and visible sign of what had always been an inward and spiritual grace of his ministry. Afterwards, when he had retired from the mission and was talking on that Spring morning he spoke of this matter with feeling. It had arisen out of the question as to how far he had felt it needful to reduce the amount of credal belief to which he felt himself committed. The communion, he said again, was absolutely centred to his Christian life as it was, in his view, to the Christian life in general.

'I'm high chapel if not high church' he said, 'and I firmly believe the communion table should be open, for I believe it is an evangelising as well as a sacramental event'. He added, with rather uncharacteristic sharpness; 'I'm sick to death of prohibitions and considerations of what is meant by this sacrament and who may be admitted to it'.

It was a matter touched upon in *Priestland's Progress,* the best seller produced by the BBC Religious Affairs Correspondent in 1981. There, in company with the Archbishop of Canterbury, Cardinal Hume and others, in an exploration of the meaning of this sacrament, Soper had reacted in a similar way. Now, in this talk, he went on: 'I welcome anybody who wants to come. I don't agree that the Eucharist should be seen as a fruit of unity, not a means to it. It is an occasion of dissension and separation only too often. What I want to share is the supremely dramatic and evangelical impact of communion which goes far beyond the word used, or any of the ritual appurtenances associated with it. It's physical — you stretch out your hands — it's evocative, set round with mystery. I believe more truth comes to people in such moments through such acts than through rational thinking.'

On the matter of Christian belief in general, he clearly had not moved from the position he had expressed in the *Advocacy of the Gospel* many years before. 'When I began my ministry, I was trying to hold on to about three hundred and fifty different theological propositions...' That had changed, even by the time of that writing. He recognised few truths; but these were sufficient to hold him strongly enough to enable him to be dubious about many others. That was the time when he was saying; 'I rest on this confidence; that Jesus is the way, the truth and the life. On these rations — iron rations if you like, I think I shall probably go the rest of my journey.' Now, at least thirty five years later, he said: 'I think a Christian now should learn a great truth which comes from the

Orthodox church — the doctrine of economy — the virtue of having few but simple basic beliefs. If you challenge me to what things I am prepared to maintain without equivocation I would place first what I said years ago and I have always said: that Jesus is the way, the truth and the life. But you must permit me to interpret those words in all kinds of ways which may not be semantically obvious or even comprehensible to other people.'

How far have his ideas in general really changed with the passage of time? It would be easy to conclude that they have in fact changed very little, and that he has been saying all along the same things, although clothing them with much variety of expression. In other words, the ideas have remained static; but their presentation has been variable. He has claimed, and in this talk did so again, to be essentially a simple man, with the implication that he needed few fundamental truths to get along with.

But this is a surface impression. The more Donald Soper is spoken with, preferably privately and without the atmosphere of argument, the clearer it becomes that he takes trouble to feed his mind, and to keep it contemporary, as well as expressing views. The books upon his desk that morning in Kingsway included, for instance, the latest from Hans Küng, an exploratory theologian if ever there was one.

Another occupational hazard is the temptation to use the same ready answers when faced with the same questions over and over again, all of which can add up to a suggestion of light-weight thinking. But such is not really the case with Soper. He would not have survived the very severe challenges to belief and conduct which the years had brought to him if it was so. That he remains basically a simple man may well be true; but equally true is that it is a simplicity which is strong enough to resist the demolition men of the more extravagant theological thinking of recent years. As he said in an interview, at a time when demolition was more of a novelty than it is now: 'What do I think about the death of God? I don't know. I hadn't heard he was unwell.'

On such a question as church unity he shows however some

change of stance because the situation itself seems to have altered. 'For many people church unity is no longer an issue.' At least on a superficial level, many of the divisions between churches have been overcome. Coming together in shared worship, and a general friendliness, have satisfied the demands of people who often go no further than that and have been satisfied with these meagre victories. But they have in so doing, missed the call to go deeper. That is one attitude. Another is that, within the last few years, what was endemic in the last century has begun to emerge in this — the rise of non-rational creeds, and a great many enthusiastic believers now no longer care in the least about church unity because they are starting their own communities and having an enjoyable time cuddling themselves. The Moral Majority people in the United States are an example. But there are many others, especially among the minority communities here. They have recognised, and accurately, sad to say, that there is no hope for them within the established main-line churches and have gone off on their own into the most ridiculous cults. So that, instead of integration, you have an even greater degree of polarisation.

So church unity has in some ways lost significance and in others changed direction. I think the emphasis has in one sense very properly moved away from attempts to say the same thing while serving the same kind of rituals, into a field which is very much more fertile, that is, into a seeking for common attitudes towards some of the outstanding moral problems of these times. I don't worry very much over whether someone wishes to say his prayers in one place, say them quietly, shout them loud, or whatever, so long as we act together in social issues.'

The increasingly shared attitude of opposition to the use of nuclear weapons by Christians of all communions was, he felt, an instance of this.

His political thinking seems to show a greater degree of change, and that towards the left, in what appears to be a reaction towards what he sees as the emergence of a new Right. The poverty which he met as a young minister has, in its cruder forms, vanished. But a new one has taken its place so that, feeling deeply about the poor among some middle class people, and about the burgeoning wealth of monetarist capitalism with its multi-national links, co-existing with massive, unemployment, he finds much to combat. But the shapes of things are changing, especially in politics, therefore, so are his views with them.

He said: 'There is a possibility of a breaking of the mould of the two party system. It may or may not happen; but I think there are two elements to be taken into consideration if it is going to happen. One is a very considerable increase in classical capitalism compared, say, with the Macmillan era. Meanwhile the Labour party has fallen between two stools. It has failed to express socialist principles and has thus divided, and I cannot see any reconciliation possible. What concerns me is that this division, with the emergence of the Social Democratic Party, is a recipe for keeping the right in power. That gives me no pleasure whatsoever'.

Whatever the state of the parties, none the less, he did not think the political structure was any longer strong enough by itself to stand up to contemporary power pressures. 'That is why', he added, 'I hold more firmly than ever the need for personal probity and personal decency, and unless you can have a political system with such things you can be lost. So I am more than ever concerned about conversion, though not in the way in which people talk of sudden change of heart, some emotional spiritual event; but conversion in response to a society which manifestly needs high moral qualities in order to succeed, and regards such qualities as inherent necessities. Unless that is a concern of the individual politician then I cannot think much of political ambitions.' One was reminded here of a talk with former Prime Minister Harold Wilson about Donald Soper. Shaking his head, Wilson remarked on that occasion that ideals of this order rarely survive the rough and tumble of political life.

He may have been right; but Donald would certainly not have thought so, nor think so now. As to democracy as a popular idea, he held, as he always has done, that democracy understood the right of people to say what they wish to say was only half the story. The other and essential half was whether the people have economic opportunities to influence the events. To the other question as to whether we have ever experienced democracy in this sense he replied: 'of course we haven't! We haven't seen the kingdom of God yet, either!'

There was an echo of the past. He used often in earlier years to condemn the practise of thinking of the kingdom in unreal terms as some kind of wonderland where sorrow and sighing would be no more, and where perpetual light would shine upon the righteous. But it was not so, he used to say: the kingdom was to be striven after here and now, and should be recognisable in the way this world could be ordered, as well as in the seeking after private spirituality. But what did he think of this matter now? Have we progressed towards this recognisable kingdom at all?

Of all the responses made in this conversation, those on this theme, seemed the least satisfactory, or at any rate out of proportion to the magnitude of the issue, as though he was wishing to present relatively minor issues in a major battle as in themselves final victories. 'I mean', he said, 'by the kingdom of God now those elements in the world in which we live which are reconcilable with the spirit and the teaching of Jesus and are the marks of victories which have been made in his name, or at least under his inspiration. For instance, slavery has been in general abolished, even though some industrial forms of it persist. Secondly, most people today have an awareness of their responsibility to animals. These appreciations are part of the kingdom of God. Furthermore, there can be no doubt that hope — and the possibility — of better conditions and a more worthwhile life on this planet have been offered to multitudes of people who live in utter hopelessness before, and the emergence of hope, even in conditions where that hope is frustrated, are parts of the kingdom of God.'

But one area where he showed no evidence in change of position was in regard to pacifism. And here it was difficult not to be impressed by the prodigious length of time he could look back over the events of this century, especially in this particular area. He has been an active participant in the pacifist cause for so long that he has come to look almost like a symbol of it. He was preaching his own singularly simple gospel of total non-violence as long ago as the twenties, and the beginning of the great anti-war emotions which eventually emerged from the tragedy of World War One. He was a close associate of those founding figures of early thirties pacifism: Sheppard, Lansbury, Vera Brittain. The rise of fascism and a second world war did not alter his views in any way. He was preaching pacifism on Tower Hill during the Battle of Britain itself. In after times he was involved from its beginnings with the campaign for nuclear disarmament, and he has seen in all the developments of the nuclear threat since then only confirmation of his fundamental belief that all violence is self destructive, and that all those that live by the sword, in whatever form manifests itself now — and they are many — will perish by it.

This is a message which has obviously assumed a tragic urgency as a situation has developed unimaginable to the early pioneers of pacifism of whom Soper is one of the few living survivors. 'Since 16 July, 1945', writes Johnathan Schell in his remarkable recent book *The Fate of the Earth* 'when the first atomic bomb was detonated.... mankind has lived with nuclear weapons in its midst. Each year the number of bombs has grown, until now there are some fifty thousand war-heads in the world. These bombs were built as weapons for war; but their significance greatly transends war and all its causes and outcomes. They grew out of history, yet they threaten to end history. They are a pit into which the whole world can fall, a nemesis of all human intentions, actions and hopes.' And he goes on to refer to the strange paralysis of will which seems to make it possible for millions of people to recognise the threat and yet to feel unable to do anything effective about it.

In so truly an awful a situation there seems a new dignity about the apparent simplicities of the position which Donald Soper has always taken, and will die holding, unaltered. 'I've lived to see that the moral claim for pacifism is immensely strengthened by the practical effects of a continuation of the policies that deny it', he says. 'I am more convinced than ever that what is wrong can never be politically right, and it is that comfort that I find necessary at times like this when the actions and attitudes of a great many people today seem no more enlightened than forty years ago. Either we bring this world to an end by the use of our nuclear power, or we bring the present order to an end, as Jesus believed it should be brought to an end, in order that a better might take its place.'

As to himself, in the evening of his days, what did he see at the end of so long a road? The answer was unadorned. 'I don't know; but "in my father's house are many mansions". I am an old man, and the more I think about the next world the more perplexed I get. But I hold to the words that "all things work together for good to them that love God"; and I try to keep my eyes fixed on what I have to do and be, by the grace of God.'

# Index